D0889772

THE PERSONALITY
OF JONATHAN SWIFT

The Personality
of Jonathan Swift

by

IRVIN EHRENPREIS

BARNES & NOBLE, Inc.
New York
METHUEN & CO. Ltd
London

First published in 1958

Reprinted, 1969
by
Barnes & Noble, Inc., New York
and
Methuen & Co. Ltd, London

Barnes & Noble SBN 389 01073 1
Methuen SBN 416 60310 6

Printed in the United States of America

TO

GEORGE SHERBURN

CONTENTS

PREFACE

My main purpose, in these essays, has been to show how Swift's personality could enter into his work: the topics which raise the hottest tempers when Swift is discussed belong to the region where biography meets criticism. I have also tried to undermine some of the false traditions concerning Swift. The most widespread – that of a secret marriage – I have attacked only sideways, in the first chapter, by showing that for a man of his nature a companionship without sexuality or wedlock was probably the deepest satisfying attachment he could form; but the heart of this chapter is the attempt to explain in general Swift's treatment of women. His politics and his religion I have also touched on indirectly, the first as it relates to his philosophy of history and the second as it affects *Gulliver's Travels* and the so-called scatological poems; and again those problems appear only as aspects of other inquiries. The allegations of obscenity and madness – two issues as controversial as any involving Swift – I have taken as the central questions of the second and sixth chapters. The third and seventh chapters deal with less sensational matters, but present a fair supply of corrective data as aids to the understanding of Swift's character. Unfortunately, the narrative of the seventh overlaps, in some ways, the argument of the sixth; however, I felt it was worth suffering that fault in order to set the question of insanity in the sharp light which it needs.

Although I have followed the original spelling and punctuation in all quotations, I have modernized the use of capitals and italics. I have indicated omissions in the middle of a quotation but not at the opening or the close.

For comprehensive improvements of my scholarship or style, I am indebted to Professor Oliver W. Ferguson of Duke University, Professor George Sherburn of Harvard University, Mr Mark Spilka of the University of Michigan, and Mr Jonathan Wordsworth of Exeter College, Oxford. For more specialized assistance I am indebted to Professor H. W. Donner of the University of Uppsala, Professor R. B. Gottfried of Indiana University, Mr Max Novak of the University of California at Los Angeles, Dr Theodore Redpath of Trinity College, Cambridge, Mr Edward L. Ruhe of Cornell University, and Miss Kathleen Williams of the University College of South Wales.

Chapter One was published in the September 1955 issue of *PMLA*; Chapter Three, in the January 1948 issue of *Studies in Philology*; and Chapter Five in the December 1957 issue of *PMLA*.

I am deeply grateful to the John Simon Guggenheim Memorial Foundation for a fellowship under which I wrote most of this book.

I. E.

Chapter One

WOMEN

Nobody has yet remarked the amazing consistency which framed Swift's relations with women. Yet the pattern need only be pointed out to be perceived, for it is recurrent, unusual (if not unique), and extraordinarily illuminating. Naturally enough, it is a pattern which originates in the author's childhood.

Swift was born in Dublin about eight months after the death of his father: he came – as Mrs Pilkington says he told her – in just 'time enough to save his mother's credit'.[1] Already fatherless, he lost his mother in a year or two, according to an incredible tale which we nevertheless have from his own pen. Having been handed over to a nurse, he endeared himself to her so thoroughly that when the woman had to visit England on her own business, she smuggled Jonathan along. At his mother's request, she kept him in England for almost three years, after which the child was considered old enough to risk a return voyage.[2] But once restored to the maternal clasp, he was soon torn loose again. At the age of about six or seven he was sent away to school in Kilkenny, and from there he went to the university when he was fourteen. Meanwhile, Mrs Swift had gone, with her

[1] Letitia Pilkington, *Memoirs* (London, 1928), p. 57.
[2] See Swift's autobiographical fragment, printed as the Appendix to Deane Swift, *An Essay upon . . . Dr Jonathan Swift* (London, 1755), pp. 38-39.

only other child, Jane, to live in her native town of Leicester. Yet Swift continued to regard his mother with undiminished affection and respect. Her death, though in the fullness of years and preceded by a tedious illness, shook and depressed him profoundly.[1]

Whatever the original facts may be, this is the essential pattern – the lonely life of a fatherless child (probably not robust) – which is later reflected in Swift's relations with women. When he was twenty-eight years old, for example, he began to correspond with a young woman named Jane Waring. She was the eldest child of the widow of Roger Waring, Archdeacon of Dromore; and Swift had probably first come to know her family during his years at Trinity College, Dublin, when the Archdeacon was still alive.[2] Now he had returned to Ireland to become a priest in the Established Church. His first parish was Kilroot, on the far north-east coast, in a region where the small, if dominant, class of Anglicans like himself was engulfed by a population of Roman Catholics and Presbyterians: he felt lonely and cut off. The parish of Kilroot lay far out on the great bay of Belfast Loch; Swift could ride a horse from Kilroot to the city of Belfast in a few hours, and he probably did so often. At any rate, his letters indicate a renewed and serious acquaintance with Jane Waring. She was about twenty-one when the affair began; her health was poor; and she lived with her mother in Belfast. In his correspondence, Swift called her Varina.

Although the earliest letter preserved is from April 1696, it concerns an engagement which had obviously been for

[1] See Swift's *Works*, ed. John Nichols (London, 1808), X, 105.
[2] H. B. Swanzey, *Succession Lists of the Diocese of Dromore* (Belfast, 1933), pp. 42-43.

some time an unfailing source of heady conversation between them. Varina apparently considered his proposal ill-timed. She could not see herself enjoying life either in Kilroot or on Swift's income. But their affair soon reached its crisis when Swift was invited to rejoin his English patron, Sir William Temple, in whose home he had spent five years, on and off, after leaving Trinity College. He was tired of Kilroot and welcomed the prospect of an improved status. Under this happy stimulus, he begged Varina to make a decisive gesture and engage herself to marry him when his circumstances permitted that step. He would then reject Temple's offer, stay in Ireland, and work away at his ecclesiastical career: 'I desire nothing of your fortune; you shall live where and with whom you please till my affairs are settled to your desire, and in the meantime I will push my advancement with all the eagerness and courage imaginable, and do not doubt to succeed.' If she preferred to remain sickly and single, and he left the kingdom before she was his, he would 'endure the utmost indignities of fortune rather than ever return again, though the King would send me back his Deputy'.[1]

Swift did leave Ireland without Varina; King William did not send him back as Lord Deputy; but three years later, having endured something less than the utmost indignities of fortune, he returned. Sir William Temple had died, and Swift had been appointed prebendary of St Patrick's Cathedral, Dublin, and Vicar of Laracor, a union of parishes between fifteen and twenty miles from the capital. His total income was almost £250 a year, and he was thirty-two years old.

[1] Swift's *Correspondence*, ed. F. E. Ball (London, 1910-14), I, 18-19. (Cited below as Ball.)

The correspondence with Varina continued, but the tone of it perceptibly altered. As her demurrals softened, his stipulations hardened. It was no longer with him a question of her physical health. Her family, her manners, and her character were scrutinized. Unless she sharply rearranged her style of life, he could not hold to his side of their understanding. When a mutual friend warned Swift of the effect his tepid attitude might have, the supposed suitor responded as tranquilly as to a weather forecast: 'You mention a dangerous rival for an absent lover; but I must take my fortune. If the report proceeds, pray inform me.'[1] He was not languishing for Varina.

But the young lady could not accept the new attitude. She revived the question of their engagement; and when Swift's reply seemed evasive, she wrote again, bringing forward such questions as, Why had his manner changed since his arrival in Ireland? Had he fallen in love with somebody else? Why was he curious about Varina's own finances? and, When was he coming to see her?

Swift's rejoinder shows that, having lost interest, he had tried to let her down with a minimum of discomfort. But, since polite vagueness had proved unsatisfactory, he was ready to be blunt. His alteration, such as it was, had been occasioned by her indifference to prayers for her amendment. She had neglected her health and manners as much as ever, clinging to the bad associations of her remarried mother. As to the rival sweetheart, he swore (without actually denying her existence) that it was not thoughts of one which had changed his attitude. Her fortune was relevant, however, because she expected to live more handsomely

[1] Ball, I, 30.

than he could afford, even with the addition of her income
of 'almost a hundred pounds a year'. No, he would not visit
Belfast, since his duties confined him to Dublin. The letter
ends in a cascade of challenges which, so far as is known,
effectively stifled the relationship: 'Have you such an inclination to my person and humour, as to comply with my
desires and way of living, and endeavour to make us both
as happy as you can? Will you be ready to engage in those
methods I shall direct for the improvement of your mind,
so as to make us entertaining company for each other,
without being miserable when we are neither visiting nor
visited? Can you bend your love and esteem and indifference
to others the same way as I do mine?'[1]

Although Varina was seven years his junior, the sub-
missiveness which Swift expected would have been more
appropriate in a daughter than a mistress. Earlier, he had
himself been entirely obedient, but he had now become
arrogant. Neither attitude is that of a prospective partner in
marriage. On the contrary, in his bold replies to the fatherless Varina, Swift seemed to betray a remarkable degree of
independence. Apparently her defects were a foil to another
woman's virtues; and Swift could be so short with one
because he knew how readily the other would live in his
way, welcome his tutelage, cheer his despair, and abide with
him, never requiring what Varina did – marriage.

Esther Johnson (the other woman) was young, frail, and
the elder of two fatherless children when Swift met her. She
lived on Sir William Temple's estate; her mother worked
for Temple's sister, and her father had been his steward. She
was seven or eight years old the first time Swift saw her.

---

[1] Ball, I, 34-35.

He helped to educate the child, and her handwriting always resembled his, a source of later confusion. In 1696, when he returned to Sir William Temple, she was fifteen – seven years younger than Varina, fourteen years younger than Swift. Her health had improved, and she began to put on weight. To the eyes of her friend she soon seemed one of the most beautiful and agreeable young women in London, her hair blacker than a raven and every feature in perfection. 'She had a gracefulness', said Swift, 'somewhat more than human in every motion, word, and action. Never was so happy a conjunction of civility, freedom, easiness, and sincerity.'[1]

But Esther had more durable charms than good manners and a well-turned figure. These gifts, which Swift could neither discover nor inspire in Varina, may be summed up as pliability and masculinity. 'The little disguises, and affected contradictions of your sex,' he had warned Varina, 'were all . . . infinitely beneath persons of your pride and mine.'[2] Esther showed less petulance. In arguments she was never stubborn, and usually treated those who were in a way that encouraged their leaning: 'When she saw any of the company very warm in a wrong opinion [said Swift], she was more inclined to confirm them in it than oppose them. The excuse she commonly gave when her friends asked the reason, was, That it prevented noise, and saved time.'[3]

Not only did Esther eschew Varina's romantic affectations and womanish airs; she tried to be independent, well-read, and courageous, and yet to preserve the refinement and softness that became a lady. Once when she was living in an

---

[1] Swift, 'On the Death of Mrs Johnson', in John Hayward's Nonesuch *Swift* (London, 1934), p. 726. (Cited below as Hayward.)
[2] Ball, I, 20.   [3] Hayward, p. 733.

isolated neighbourhood, a gang of burglars tried to break into the house. There was a boy among the servants but no man. While the other females and he withdrew half dead from fear, Esther tiptoed to her dining-room window, carrying a pistol. She wore a black hood to prevent her from being seen in the darkness. Quietly raising the sash, she aimed straight at one of the thieves and shot him so neatly that he died the next day.

Esther enjoyed conversation and made no display of shyness. She spoke in a pleasant voice and simple words, never hesitating except out of modesty before new faces. But she did not speak much at a time, and refused absolutely to discuss fashions, scandal, or immoral topics. Her visitors were more commonly men than women, particularly clergy-men. One reason was that she enjoyed reading and talking about books which women seldom read: history, especially of Greece and Rome, though also that of France and England; books of travel; the higher levels of recent and contemporary poetry and essays. She understood Platonic and Epicurean philosophy, could point out the errors in Hobbes' materialism, and had good taste in literature generally. Thus she accurately reflected the leanings of her instructor.

Esther Johnson left her mother's home in 1701, after her younger sister was married.[1] At Swift's invitation, she and a friend named Rebecca Dingley moved to Dublin. She never saw England again except for a few months' trip in 1708. Although Swift did not marry her, and normally met her only in the presence of third parties – Rebecca Dingley,

[1] The marriage of Stella's sister is mentioned as a very recent event in a letter by Lady Giffard, 14 July 1700 (B.M. MS. Eg. 1705, f. 25 – a sentence omitted from the published text).

most of the time – she became his dearest, most intimate companion. From 1702 to 1714 Swift spent something like half his time in England. Yet he corresponded frequently with Esther Johnson, and at last kept a diary which he sent her every ten or fifteen days, so that she often knew more of his doings than his friends in London.

One event that took place in 1708, he may hardly have mentioned to her. This was the beginning of his interest in another woman named Esther, seven years younger than her and twenty-one years younger than Swift. Esther Vanhomrigh was the daughter of a prosperous merchant who had risen to be lord mayor of Dublin and commissary-general of the armed forces in Ireland. He had died late in 1703, leaving a widow and four children, of whom Esther (who also had bad health) was the eldest. Her mother migrated to London with the children four years later, and Swift must have met the family soon, through mutual friends. He took to visiting the Vanhomrighs' for meals, parties, conversation, or simply loafing. Esther quickly caught his interest, and he began suggesting books for her to read and acquaintances for her to drop. He called the fatherless girl Hessy at first, but later nicknamed her Vanessa, a compound of the first syllables of her two names.

Vanessa's mother lived with less thrift than show, in a rather fast set of stylish young ladies, state functionaries, and smart gentlemen of leisure. Their regular social amusements were anything from card parties to sightseeing trips, but talk was their continual recreation. Thus Swift's attendance must have been a blessing to an ambitious hostess, for he was not only a well-known author and on his way to becoming an influence on the heads of the English government; he was also one of the most brilliant conversationalists of his day.

Vanessa accepted Dr Swift's fatherly attentions with a keen though hardly filial enjoyment. For his part, he preferred her company to that of her family or friends; he liked to drink coffee with her or eat an orange and sugar in a room apart; he disapproved, though, of her attitude toward himself and of her laziness. Gradually he extended his didactic methods, until he reached the point of sending her an analysis of her shortcomings. As any reader of that analysis can see, she adopted his political sympathies out of an enthusiasm for her teacher rather than his subjects. It is equally plain that her indiscretion disturbed him more than her indolence: 'I have corrected all her faults; but . . . she is incorrigibly idle and lazy – thinks the world made for nothing but perpetual pleasure; and the deity she most adores is Morpheus. . . . She makes me of so little consequence that it almost distracts me. She will bid her sister go downstairs before my face, for she has "some private business with the Doctor".'[1]

For almost three years more, their casual but dangerous liaison grew stronger. Soon Vanessa began to save the notes and letters which Swift wrote to her when he left town. Then, perhaps with more ominous intent, she began to retain copies of her own letters to him. Swift had grasped that he meant more to Vanessa than he should, and he tried to shift their friendship to a less intimate plane. As he pulled back, however, she characteristically stepped out, until a clean break seemed his only sensible exit. Swift could not bring himself to take this desperate remedy.

In 1713 Swift was made Dean of St Patrick's Cathedral,

[1] A. Martin Freeman, *Vanessa and Her Correspondence with Jonathan Swift* (London, 1921), pp. 68-69. (Cited below as Freeman.)

Dublin. When he went back to be installed, he sent a brief letter to Vanessa, which opens conventionally enough, yet closes on the exact note he would have liked her to keep: 'It is impossible for anybody to have more acknowledgments at heart, for all your kindness and generosity to me. . . . Pray God preserve you and make you happy and easy – and so adieu, brat.'[1] How long she was able to hold this note appears from any of the three letters she composed to him within a single week. Here is part of the second, in which she reacts to the news of his bad fit of vertigo: 'I have done all that was possible to hinder myself from writing to you till I heard you were better, for fear of breaking my promise, but 'twas all in vain; for had [I] vowed neither to touch pen, ink or paper, I certainly should have had some other invention. Therefore I beg you won't be angry with me for doing what is not in my power to avoid.'[2]

Wheedling and coercion of this sort chilled Swift. He responded with an informative but not very tender report of his activities. Unfortunately this only whetted her appetite for contention. 'I had your last spleenatic letter', Swift was forced to reply. 'I told you when I left England, I would endeavour to forget everything there, and would write as seldom as I could.'[3]

But politics dragged him back to London in a few months, and the treadmill went on. Soon Vanessa had a more urgent claim on him than her infatuation; her mother died in 1714 and left her children a tangled estate, weighted with many foolish debts. Swift had great experience of legal and financial muddles; so he quickly assisted Vanessa with both money and advice: but he still evaded her emotions.

[1] Freeman, pp. 78-79.　　[2] Freeman, p. 87.　　[3]Freeman, p. 90.

Then Queen Anne died in August 1714, and Swift's leaders slid from the height of power into a morass of prosecutions. He hurried to Dublin to secure his deanery, planning only a short stay. Instead, he remained twelve years in Ireland.

For a woman of ordinary composure this event would have ended the affair, especially since Swift wrote that he would avoid her if she tried to visit her native city. But the last and most miserable twist of the melodrama lay before them. Vanessa packed up her debts and moved with her family to a house outside Dublin. She begged Swift to call on her, and he replied, 'I would not have gone . . . to see you for all the world. I ever told you you wanted discretion.' He promised to pay a brief visit when she came to town, and ended, 'Nor shall you know where I am till I come, and then I will see you. A fig for your letters and messages. Adieu.'[1]

Vanessa was now in the habit of using her genuine legal tangles and her bad health as a lever to pry Swift out of his diffidence. Her addresses became impassioned, then distracted. The anguish prolonged itself from weeks to months, and finally to years, but without substantial change. Swift wrote to her rarely, elliptically, or sometimes in French, asking her also to be oblique, and suggesting codes for them to use – so anxious was he about the possibility of scandal. Yet at thirty-two she could still write to Swift (who was now fifty-three),

> 'Tis now ten long, long weeks since I saw you, and in all that time I have never received but one letter from you, and a little note with an excuse. Oh – – – how have you forgot me! You endeavour by severities to force me from you; nor can I blame

---

[1] Freeman, pp. 100-101.

you. . . . Yet I cannot comfort you. . . . Put my passion under the utmost restraint, send me as distant from you as the earth will allow, yet you cannot banish those charming ideas, which will ever stick by me whilst I have the use of memory. Nor is the love I bear you only seated in my soul, for there is not a single atom of my frame that is not blended with it.[1]

From such a struggle only one release was possible, but it did not come until 1723, when Swift was fifty-six and Vanessa thirty-five. He remained intractable and she, possessed, until a congenitally weak constitution carried her, like the other Vanhomrighs, into a premature grave.

We should know better than to blame either member of this dismal relationship. Swift was looking for rational friends who would respect conventions. His 'Letter to a Young Lady, on Her Marriage' includes many hints of what he desired. The docility he expected, though, could never have worn well on a woman who felt independent of him. A pattern of fatherless girls much younger than himself, and all in bad health, can be linked to his own posthumous birth, his early lack of an immediate family, and his constant wrestling with illness. The role of parent gave him a double pleasure: first, he could provide his beloved with that guidance and warmth which he himself had missed and therefore valued intensely; secondly, he could make up to himself for the inadequacy of his childhood, since the women he chose had needs much like his own, so that (without realizing it) he might imagine that he was reaching back into the 1670's and in an odd but vivid way treat the other person as deputy for his younger self. This was one reason – though far from the only reason – that he praised

---

[1] Freeman, pp. 127-8.

in women traits often classified as masculine: these facilitated his identification with them. Thus, when Swift, in the poem he wrote to praise Vanessa, gave her mythological blessings at her birth, he was careful to include the following lines, in which Athene, having been tricked into thinking the babe is male,

> *sows within her tender mind*
> *Seeds long unknown to womankind,*
> *For manly bosoms chiefly fit,*
> *The seeds of knowledge, judgment, wit.*
> *Her soul was suddenly endu'd*
> *With justice, truth and fortitude;*
> *With honour, which no breath can stain,*
> *Which malice must attack in vain;*
> *With open heart and bounteous hand.*[1]

That these girls should also have been eldest children confirms the bond with his infancy. While Swift's mother first lost and then left Jonathan, she kept with her the only other child in the family: Jane, his elder sister (by two years), and the namesake of Miss Waring. When he was not supplying his woman friends with the father he would have liked to have, Swift was regaining in them the sister whom he had missed.[2]

Sexuality and marriage were not elements in such a scheme as Swift's, and a stubborn person like Varina spoiled the gratifying sameness of his fantasy. As for Vanessa, so long as she put up with his caprices, showered him with affection, and took his advice seriously, he could not discard her; and

---

[1] Swift's *Poems,* ed. Sir Harold Williams (Oxford, 1937), II, 693. (Cited below as *Poems.*)

[2] For this analysis of the connection between Swift's sister and his woman friends, I am indebted to Dr Phyllis Greenacre's *Swift and Carroll* (New York, 1955), p. 40 and passim.

the strength of her passion added a lure which Esther John-son either did not feel or did not show. Why Vanessa was unable to give Swift up is no riddle: she met him a few years after her father died, and pursued him soon after her mother died; there was a powerful need for a parent mixed in with the other ingredients of her yearning. But one can hardly accuse him of misleading a woman who at twenty-six had tracked him from London to Dublin against his express cautions, and who pursued him frantically nine years more. Since their relationship remained static during that long finale, and since Vanessa, though the eldest of the four Vanhomrigh children, was the longest-lived, it would be absurd to blame him for her death. Nor was it unnatural of Swift to suppose that a girl who had accepted so many conditions could be brought to accept all; it was just very naïve of him. And Vanessa certainly had other employment than watering her couch with tears. Her own letters had been written wildly, while she beat herself into agonies that might move Swift. She did have resources of her own – a bright, curious mind, a circle of interesting friends, a home furnished and maintained with considerable luxury. She was in misery often, but not continually. Nobody could make groans her meat for nine unbroken years.

Vanessa's death unsettled Swift's stability, partly because he had quarrelled with her some time before, so decisively that they did not meet afterwards. He set off on a tremen-dous excursion alone through the south of Ireland, rejoining his friends only after months had passed. One of those friends, Esther Johnson, may well have known about Swift's tie with Vanessa; but her devotion remained untouched. She had enjoyed immeasurable advantages over her rival.

Swift, addressing her as Stella at least since 1719, had openly acknowledged her as his best friend. Beyond this, he had found her increasingly a support as well as a charge. She had nursed him through his diseases, presided at his entertainments, heard out his daily complaints, and had thrown a motherly screen between his uneasy nature and the haze of annoyances which beset him:

> When on my sickly couch I lay,
> Impatient both of night and day . . .
> Then Stella ran to my relief
> With chearful face, and inward grief . . .
> No cruel master could require
> From slaves employ'd for daily hire
> What Stella by her friendship warm'd,
> With vigour and delight perform'd.[1]

The relation between them had not stood still. It had altered so that she ultimately made him almost as good a parent as he made her. Though generally indifferent to the stubbornness of others in argument, she had appeared to Swift 'very angry with some whom she much esteemed for sometimes falling into that infirmity'.[2] This is his standard phraseology when he means to point to himself. Stella must have known when she could, without risk, expose him to her anger; and he must have recognized the justice of her feeling each time. Here was another evidence of the motherly instinct in Stella which hardly showed at all in Vanessa, who never babied Swift.

The link with Stella was therefore strong. It lasted serenely to the end of her days, and perhaps it even touched Swift's most popular book, *Gulliver's Travels*. Lemuel Gulliver,

---

[1] *Poems*, II, 726.   [2] Hayward, p. 733.

while voyaging, formed only one deep emotional relationship with a female – a girl whom he first met when she was
a child of nine. Yet in a short time she grew so fond of him
that she left her family to live with him, and he called her
his 'little nurse'. When he grew sick, she cared for him;
although many years his junior, she treated him exactly like
a baby, helping him on and off with his clothes. He answered
her affection with equal affection, but never forgot that she
was a child. Their intimacy was cut off when he took a sea
voyage to another country. Yet as he realized he was leaving
her, probably forever, he wailed consciously and patheti-
cally, 'How often did I then wish my self with my dear
Glumdalclitch, from whom one single hour had so far
divided me!'[1]

I mean of course the young giantess on whose father's
farm Gulliver was first discovered in Brobdingnag. While
the farmer, by his avarice and insensitivity, only alienated
Gulliver, and the wife screamed at the tiny castaway as
though he were a toad, while one son almost dropped him
to his death, and the baby tried to bite off his head, Glumdalclitch was of a different composition:

> . . . a daughter of nine years old, a child of toward parts for
> her age, very dextrous at her needle, and skilful in dressing her
> baby. Her mother and she contrived to fit up the baby's cradle
> for me against night. . . . This young girl was so handy, that
> after I had once or twice pulled off my cloaths before her, she
> was able to dress and undress me, though I never gave her that
> trouble when she would let me do either my self. She made
> me seven shirts, and some other linen . . . and these she con-
> stantly washed for me with her own hands. . . . She was very

[1] *Gulliver's Travels*, ed. Sir Harold Williams (London, 1926), p. 191. (Cited
below as *Gulliver*.)

good natur'd, and not above forty foot high, being little for her age. . . . To her I chiefly owe my preservation in that country: We never parted while I was there. . . .[1]

Swift has achieved the quaint fantasy of a mother forty feet tall but young enough to be his daughter: a behemoth against whom he could offer no resistance, yet whose entire life was consecrated to his service; a source of unflagging affection starting up suddenly, with no effort on his part, and to which he need have made no return. How improbable her character seems! What nine-year-old ever deserted her family in order to stay indefinitely with a pet which she had owned for three months? This is not a portrait or even a caricature. It is a reverie, playing about the archetypes of the women to whom Swift felt drawn; and while there may be allusions to Esther Johnson in the fantasy, they are mixed and distorted.

The giantess possessed one happy attribute which Stella lacked: her physical health was unbroken. But by the time *Gulliver's Travels* appeared, Mrs Johnson was passing into her final illness. Several times in 1726 her life seemed all but lost; in 1727 she never had, said Swift, 'a day's health'. In the prayers which he wrote for her during the last season of her distress, he laments his own desolation: 'Forgive the sorrow and weakness of those among us, who sink under the grief and terror of losing so dear and useful a friend.'[2]

Late in the evening of her death he sat alone, sick in his room, and put down memoirs of her life and character. About midnight he stopped and went to bed. The second night he went on, but his head ached so that he could not add much. The third night was her funeral, which his own

---

[1] *Gulliver*, pp. 124-5.   [2] Hayward, p. 738.

illness mercifully would not permit him to attend. But the deanery faced the cathedral; therefore, he moved into a special room, where he might not see the light in the church, 'just over against the window of my bed-chamber'.[1] As the holy office proceeded, he continued to memorialize his friend. But he knew too much for the spare hours of three single nights to contain; so he added paragraph on paragraph later, as he found time: 'She had the esteem and friendship of all who knew her, and the universal good-report of all who ever heard of her, without one exception, if I am told the truth by those who keep general conversation. Which character . . . must be rather imputed to her great modesty, gentle behaviour, and inoffensiveness, than to her superior virtues.'[2] Yet under the elegy of praise a darker grief is heard, like that which Swift expressed when his mother died: 'I have now lost my barrier between me and death.'[3]

[1] Hayward, p. 727.   [2] Hayward, p. 734.
[3] Swift's *Works*, ed. John Nichols, X, 105.

Chapter Two

OBSCENITY

I

In all satire', said Wordsworth, 'there will be found a spice of malignity.'[1] Though this postulate may do less to explain Swift's success as a satirist than to explain Wordsworth's failure, it is a commonplace of shallow thought on the subject: find the malignity, and you have accounted for the satire. But in dealing with Swift, it is one thing to say that the man himself was eccentric – he was, though no more so than many people whom everybody knows. It is another thing to claim that his literary works are spoiled by shortcomings which are traceable to his character. There is no point in labelling him as this or that type of neurotic unless one can use the classification to understand his achievement. If the labelling conceals his achievement, it has been worse than useless.

Swift had in fact the classic traits of a compulsive personality. He made lists, he collected books, he saved money, he kept himself unusually clean; he was often obsessional. Since many scientists and literary scholars are in the same way compulsively neat, it is hardly necessary to apologize for Swift. A man's character undoubtedly affects his style and his choice of subject-matter. So we find that Swift

[1] Letter of 21 March 1796, to William Mathews.

29

worried about consistency in spelling; he praised women for cleanliness; he published pamphlets against a debased coinage. Samuel Johnson, whose character is similar to Swift's, occupied himself with compiling a dictionary – an excellent task for anybody who likes making lists and collecting things. If a critic decided that Johnson's dictionary would have to be bad because the author was preoccupied with words, or that Swift's pamphlets must fail because the writer worried about money, he might be quoted but he would not be read.

It is a fair question whether Swift's flaws or virtues as a writer are linked to his personality. That there must be some connection, I quite believe. But while there are millions of tidy, collecting, list-making, picture-straightening, obsessional, compulsive personalities, there are not millions of Swifts. Merely to classify him in a psychological category is to do little toward evaluating his art. Though Johnson and Swift, for instance, shared many traits of character, they have almost opposing effects as authors. The genius of an artist, says Lionel Trilling,

> may be defined in terms of his faculties of perception, representation, and realization, and in these terms alone. It can no more be defined in terms of neurosis than can his power of walking and talking, or his sexuality. The use to which he puts his power, or the manner and style of his power, may be discussed with reference to his particular neurosis, and so may such matters as the untimely diminution or cessation of its exercise. But its essence is irreducible. It is, as we say, a gift.
>
> We are all ill: but even a universal sickness implies an idea of health. Of the artist we must say that whatever elements of neurosis he has in common with his fellow mortals, the one part of him that is healthy, by any conceivable definition of

health, is that which gives him the power to conceive, to plan, to work, and to bring his work to a conclusion.[1]

Swift hardly requires a defence against the charge of pornography: he is not accused of stirring up the reader's sexual feelings in order to titillate them. But he has been accused of avoiding any humorous reference to the sexual act. Nevertheless, he does supply examples of what might be called dirty jokes. Encouraging Stella to exercise, he complains that Irish ladies never walk, 'as if their legs were of no use, but to be *laid aside*'.[2] Or he tells her the hour of an appointment with Oxford, 'at four, afternoon, when I will open my business to him; which expression I would not use if I were a woman'.[3] Or he ridicules the new whale-bone petticoats, 'a woman here may hide a moderate gallant under them'.[4] Since the relations between Swift and Stella, though not involving either marriage or sexual intercourse, were essentially domestic, such quips need no more apology than the racy repartee of any intimate friends. Middleton Murry objects that this freedom ends with the *Journal to Stella*.[5] Apart from the fact that he is mistaken, it seems an odd grievance that a man should have stopped making smutty remarks after he was forty-six. Furthermore, since no additional letters to Stella are extant, and since Swift limited himself, in such jesting, to special friends or special circumstances, it would not be extraordinary if his later sallies were lost. Finally, I doubt that an Anglican priest

---

[1] 'Art and Neurosis', in *The Liberal Imagination* (New York, Doubleday Anchor Books, 1953), p. 177.

[2] *Journal to Stella*, ed. Sir Harold Williams (Oxford, 1948), p. 270. (Cited below as *Journal*.)

[3] *Journal*, p. 41.   [4] *Journal*, p. 409.

[5] *Jonathan Swift* (London, 1954), p. 441. (Cited below as Murry.)

wants his character defended on the grounds that he talked bawdy in middle age.

Certainly Swift is coarse. He often uses the plain language which polite conversation does not tolerate. Here he is telling a riddle to an archdeacon, for him to try it on a bishop:

> Tell the Bishop of Clogher that Dilly Ashe had a slovenly way of pissing as he lay in bed. I desire to know what sort of stone that was, make him guess, but I will tell you. It is lay piss lazily: *lapis lazuli*.[1]

This again is intimate chatter, and now between two old friends, both men; so we may approve it as a normal example of eighteenth-century freedom of speech. It is hardly stylish today to condemn a man for using a Biblical vocabulary.

The real fault which critics complain of is obscenity in another sense: a preoccupation with bodily decay, with sex, and with filth, when those elements have no artistic function. One feels, certain critics say, that only Swift's neurotic personality could account for the fleshly squalors of his writing. It is usual to support this attitude by two assumptions: that Swift's sexual behaviour was sinister, and that his life evolved steadily toward madness. Since I have already argued one of these issues, and shall dispose of the other in a later chapter, may I suggest here that neither assumption appears valid. Swift's attachment to Stella seems comprehensible and must have been deeply satisfying. He did not go slowly insane. If we can find that there is sound and effective literary method in the motifs alleged to be objectionable, we shall have dealt with the critics on their own basis.

[1] Ball, II, 380.

Other writers – especially Miss Kathleen Williams and Professor R. M. Frye – have explained the significance of the filth-and-decay motifs in *Gulliver*.[1] But this book has stood generally outside the central attack. 'Swift's poems about women', says Aldous Huxley, 'are more ferocious than his prose about the Yahoos' –

> Read (with a bottle of smelling-salts handy, if you happen to be delicately stomached) . . . *A Beautiful Young Nymph going to Bed*. . . . nothing short of the most violent love or the intensest loathing could possibly account for so obsessive a preoccupation with the visceral and excrementitious.[2]

George Orwell has much the same comment. He describes *A Beautiful Young Nymph going to Bed* as one of Swift's 'most characteristic works', and a prime example of how Swift 'falsifies his picture of the world by refusing to see anything in human life except dirt, folly and wickedness'.[3] Middleton Murry sounds even shriller:

> Lust is natural and wholesome compared to the feeling Swift arouses. Moreover, the horror of such a 'poem' as *A Beautiful Young Nymph going to Bed* is not confined to the nausea evoked by the hideous detail; it proceeds equally from the writer's total lack of charity, his cold brutality, towards the wretched woman who is anatomized. It is utterly inhuman.[4]

Instead of trying to work through all Swift's verses of this nature, I shall take it that the *Nymph going to Bed* represents him at his most damnable, and therefore examine that poem

[1] See especially Miss Williams' '"Animal Rationis Capax." A Study of Certain Aspects of Swift's Imagery', *ELH*, XXI (1954), 193-207; and Professor Frye's 'Swift's Yahoo and the Christian Symbols for Sin', *Journal of the History of Ideas*, XV (April, 1954), pp. 201-17.

[2] 'Swift', in *Do What You Will* (London, 1929), pp. 93-94.

[3] 'Politics vs. Literature: an Examination of Gulliver's Travels', in *Shooting an Elephant* (London, 1950), p. 81.　　　　　[4] Murry, p. 439

rather minutely. To establish its meaning, however, I shall touch more lightly on a sampling of similar works. Professor Herbert Davis, Professor Maurice Johnson, and other scholars have already expounded the social and literary principles underlying Swift's attitude; but there are biographical and historical considerations as well, which strengthen its validity.[1]

II

During the summer of 1730, Swift heard the news which probably belongs among the provocations of his most scatological satires. In June the Dean of Ferns faced an indictment for rape. Dr Thomas Sawbridge came of a clerical family in Leicestershire, and Swift could have met or heard of his father, a politicking Whig pluralist from Melton Mowbray. After taking his degree in the low-church Emmanuel College, Cambridge (B.A., 1709), Sawbridge seems to have held a Leicestershire living for three years, but was deprived in 1715. He may then have been a chaplain in the navy and later for the East India Company of Bombay. In January 1728 he was imported as an Englishman to succeed Swift's detested namesake, Jonathan Smedley, as Dean of Ferns and Leighlin in Ireland.

What honour Sawbridge may have gathered through this appointment, he easily dissipated in Dublin, two years later, when (3 February 1730) he so far impaired the morals of a young woman as to be taken up (four months later) for rape. On Tuesday, 2 June, Sawbridge was arraigned for 'forcibly

---

[1] See Professor Davis's *Stella* (New York, 1942) and Professor Johnson's *The Sin of Wit* (Syracuse, 1950). The present discussion is peculiarly indebted to Chapter IV of *The Sin of Wit*.

and feloniously ravishing' Susanna Runcard. The following Monday, although he was supposed to be tried, no evidence appeared against him, and the trial was put off a week. But again no evidence appeared; so he was acquitted. A report went out that Sawbridge would indict the girl for perjury, 'he being in the county of Wexford when she swore the rape was committed against her in the city of Dublin'.[1]

But Swift preferred to accept other information. He took the news as confirming his ordinary estimate of the government's ecclesiastical policy, and he wrote in August to the Earl of Oxford,

> There is a fellow here from England, one Sawbridge, he was last term indicted for a rape. The plea he intended was his being drunk when he forced the woman; but he bought her off. He is a dean and I name him to your Lordship, because I am confident you will hear of his being a bishop.[2]

Within a few years, and without translation to the episcopal bench, Sawbridge died. But before the summer of 1730 was over, Swift wrote a ballad about him which (for those whom its topic does not repel) deserves the status of an anthology piece: *An Excellent New Ballad: or, The True English Dean to Be Hang'd for a Rape.* The stanza form, a bouncing sestet, is that of Gay's song, 'When young at the bar', from *The Beggar's Opera*; and Swift may be alluding to the words which Polly sings in the play: she says that though, as a bar maid, she did no more than kiss her usual customers, Macheath's

> *kiss was so sweet, and so closely he pressed,*
> *That I languished and pined till I granted the rest.*

[1] I have combined the accounts in various London newspapers of 13, 16, 23 and 27 June 1730.   [2] Ball, IV, 161-2.

35

In all of Swift's stanzas the final couplet rhymes on 'rape';
and the theme is the successive efforts of Sawbridge to find a
woman who will neither yield too easily nor resist with
success – Mrs Runcard, by implication, gets small pity. A
few couplets will give the spirit of the poem:

> *A holier priest ne'er was wrapt up in crape,*
> *The worst you can say, he committed a rape. . . .*
> *If maidens are ravish't, it is their own choice,*
> *Why are they so willful to struggle with men?*
> *If they would but lye quiet, and stifle their voice,*
> *No devil nor dean could ravish 'em then. . . .*[1]

To enlarge Swift's sense of outrage, there existed the
recent English case of Colonel Francis Charteris, cheat and
usurer, who had tricked his way into a fortune and married
his daughter to an earl. In February 1730 he was convicted
of rape but soon received the king's pardon. Swift's serious
implication seems that corrupted England naturally presents
the Irish clergy with agents of corruption: when politics
override all morality, an established church has no means
of maintaining its virtue. By the same figure, Swift complains that the victimized hierarchy is assisting its seducer.
It may not be an irrelevance that when the 'dean', in Swift's
ballad, tried to rape an Englishwoman, she 'bustled and
strugled, and made her escape'.

Overlaying the ethical tendency of Swift's 'unprintable'
poems, is set his loathing for the stale conventions of love
songs in his own time and in the preceding century. He
ridicules the 'mythological imagery, unconvincing shep-
herds, and fatuous colloquies' of pastoral, Petrarchan, and
Cavalier tradition.[2] He once wrote a direct (not ironic)

[1] *Poems*, II, 516, 519.   [2] Johnson, *Sin of Wit*, p. 93.

parody of their fatuous incoherence, *A Love Song. In the Modern Taste*, which begins,

> Flutt'ring spread thy purple pinions,
> Gentle Cupid o'er my heart;
> I a slave in thy dominions;
> Nature must give way to art.[1]

During the same summer as the trial of Sawbridge, Swift's young protégé, Matthew Pilkington, published *Poems on Several Occasions*. The solid pudding of this book remains an imitative lot of pastoral and amorous lyrics in the Caroline manner:

> Come hither, Mira, while the sun
> Prepares his radiant course to run,
> Come sit, my fair one, always gay,
> Inspirer of the tender lay. . . . [2]

Reading this when Sawbridge and Charteris were in the dock, and when his philanderous acquaintance Chetwode was boasting about infantile amours, a man of Swift's temper must have felt a particular disgust.[3] The tattered stuff encouraging women's preoccupations with their own adornment, outraged his taste as much as his morality. Yet one of the popular books of the year was Joseph Thurston's *The Toilette*, an imitation of the *Rape of the Lock*, and an exposition of such problems as the use of cosmetics:

> The useful powder-box be next my song,
> Friend to the old, and fav'rite of the young;
> With this the matron, venerably grey,
> Can hide the silver tokens of decay;
> With this secure can in the front-box sit,
> And court the glances of the ogling pit.
> Tho' thin her antiquated tresses lie,
> The plaist'ring powder yet deceives the eye.[4]

[1] *Poems*, II, 660.   [2] P. 96.   [3] Ball, IV, 201.   [4] Book I, p. 10.

No connoisseur of Swift would feel startled to find him hitting back, in the *Lady's Dressing-Room*, with an itemized inventory of the filthiest articles of a coquette's boudoir ('all the dirty ideas in the world in one piece', said Mrs Pilkington[1]):

> *The various combs for various uses,*
> *Fill'd up with dirt so closely fixt,*
> *No brush could force a way betwixt.*
> *A paste of composition rare,*
> *Sweat, dandriff, powder, lead and hair. . . .[2]*

III

Yet the poem which has suffered the most frantic attack will perhaps make the best example of what Swift's detractors can miss when they merely revile such issues of his imagination. In the *Nymph going to Bed*, he describes a street-walker who has come home to rest:

> *Returning at the midnight hour;*
> *Four stories climbing to her bow'r;*
> *Then, seated on a three-legg'd chair,*
> *Takes off her artificial hair:*
> *Now, picking out a crystal eye,*
> *She wipes it clean, and lays it by.*
> *Her eye-brows from a mouse's hyde,*
> *Stuck on with art on either side,*
> *Pulls off with care, and first displays 'em,*
> *Then in a play-book smoothly lays 'em.*
> *Now dextrously her plumpers draws,*
> *That serve to fill her hollow jaws.*
> *Untwists a wire; and from her gums*
> *A set of teeth completely comes.*
> *Pulls out the rags contriv'd to prop*
> *Her flabby dugs and down they drop.*

[1] Pilkington, *Memoirs*, p. 237.   [2] *Poems*, II, 526

Proceeding on, the lovely goddess
Unlaces next her steel-rib'd bodice;
Which by the operator's skill,
Press down the lumps, the hollows fill,
Up goes her hand, and off she slips
The bolsters that supply her hips.
With gentlest touch, she next explores
Her shankers, issues, running sores,
Effects of many a sad disaster;
And then to each applies a plaister.
But must, before she goes to bed,
Rub off the dawbs of white and red;
And smooth the furrows in her front,
With greasy paper stuck upon't.
She takes a bolus e'er she sleeps;
And then between two blankets creeps.[1]

Why should Swift dwell on the domestic exercises of a courtesan? The simplest answer is that as a conscientious priest he wished to discourage fornication. Some critics would snort magnificently at this suggestion. But there is abundant evidence, from those who knew him closely, of the deep veneration which Swift demonstrated for his calling. Even the frivolous Mrs Pilkington, after communion at St Patrick's, felt 'charmed to see with what a becoming piety the dean performed that solemn service', and she remarked that some persons censured him for bowing to the altar.[2] Dr Lyon reports that Swift's sermons drew a crowded audience, and that it was 'well known in Dublin' when the preaching came to his turn, every fifth Sunday.[3] Swift himself would go to prayers each morning at nine and often in the afternoon at three. In the deanery, so long as his health

[1] *Poems*, II, 581-2.
[2] Pilkington, p. 50.
[3] See Dr John Lyon, MS. notes in Hawkesworth's *Life of Swift* (item 579, M. 48. D, in the Forster Collection of the Victoria and Albert Museum), p. 75.

permitted, he read prayers to the household. But when his deafness grew too bad, his friends would withdraw about ten o'clock and he would spend some time in private devotion, using the liturgy of the Prayer Book. Dr Delany resided with Swift for more than six months before realizing that there were family prayers, because the servants were summoned to Swift's bedroom not by any special signal but simply by the clock striking the appointed hour. Delany says that the cathedral was the only church in Dublin where the sacrament was administered every Sunday. He also describes Swift at meals: 'His saying grace, both before, and after meat, was very remarkable. It was always in the fewest words that could be uttered on the occasion, but with an emphasis and fervour which every one around him saw, and felt; and with his hands clasped into one another, and lifted up to his breast, but never higher.'[1]

Swift was also old-fashioned. He disliked the new latitudinarianism and the men like Bishop Burnet who represented it. His theology and morality were conservative, out of keeping with the growing sentimentalism represented by Shaftesbury. He took the traditional view of vice. There were clergymen in his day whose tenderness toward prostitutes went further even than Middleton Murry's; but though Dean Sawbridge's lust may seem natural and wholesome to the latter, it did not amuse Dean Swift. If a Sawbridge could flourish in 1730, a Swift could wish to satirize his vice in 1731.

The reader who is willing to grant so much may still ask, Why polish the metres and spend so much craftsmanship on this dismal subject? Would a man condemning sin handle it

---

[1] [Patrick Delany,] *Observations upon Lord Orrery's Remarks* (London,1754), pp. 43-45. (Cited below as Delany.)

with such lingering care if he felt no underlying fascination? My answer is that Swift was not merely continuing the medieval Christian tradition of flaying the fornicator, but he was also ridiculing the literary fashion of praising women for their physical charms, which were often imaginary anyhow. The danger, to be sure, was social as well as literary. The men and women whom Swift knew actually did form mistaken attachments on the basis of superficial beauty; Swift constantly found marriages wrecked and infatuations flourishing because of such mistaken values. This poem has an exact pictorial equivalent in Hogarth's 'Harlot's Progress'.

But the literary fashion is more relevant: both the tradition of treating women as spiritual beings who never experience fleshly discomfort, and the related tradition of using pastoral imagery to adore women for their sensuous beauty. The ordinary lyrics of the seventeenth and eighteenth centuries make a jungle of pastoral eulogy in which females possess the etherial qualities of Dante's Beatrice and the aphrodisiac features of Homer's Circe, with no obligation to grow old or sick, no need to clean themselves, to read, or to think.

Going to Bed is after all the title of a well-known poem by Donne. Though Donne's couplets are not tetrameter but pentameter, the scene is the same – a woman stripping herself, and no hint that the love involved is innocent or lawful:

> *Off with that girdle, like heavens zone glistering,*
> *But a far fairer world incompassing.*
> *Unpin that spangled breastplate which you wear,*
> *That th'eyes of busie fooles may be stopt there.*
> *Unlace your self, for that harmonious chyme,*
> *Tells me from you, that now it is bed time.*[1]

[1] Text from John Hayward's Nonesuch *Donne* (London, 1932), p. 96.

41

If the Dean of St Patrick's would satirize fornication, I cannot blame him for copying the craftsmanship with which that sin is recommended by the Dean of St Paul's. For unless a parody is as well-turned as its model, it is a failure. The whole style of singing the bodily and angelic praises of women while ignoring their moral and intellectual aspects was hateful to Swift. When he jeers at gentlemen who love ladies for their cosmetic powers, he is jeering at a genuine and common peril in the society of his life time.

Swift wrote much in praise of women, marriage, and affection; but these works are rarely quoted. Yet the praises are candid and tender even when they are not brilliant: for example the lines (often imitated) on Biddy Floyd:

> When Cupid did his grandsire Jove intreat,
> To form some beauty by a new receit,
> Jove sent and found far in a country scene,
> Truth, innocence, good nature, look serene;
> From which ingredients, first the dext'rous boy
> Pickt the demure, the aukward, and the coy;
> The graces from the court did next provide
> Breeding, and wit, and air, and decent pride;
> These Venus cleans'd from ev'ry spurious grain
> Of nice, coquet, affected, pert, and vain.
> Jove mix'd up all, and his best clay imploy'd;
> Then call'd the happy composition, Floyd.[1]

In keeping with Swift's principles, though the verses are in the highest strain of panegyric, there is not a single reference to Mrs Floyd's appearance. All her virtues are moral or intellectual.

In view of the outraged sensibilities presented by several literary critics, it is almost incredible how few works or

[1] *Poems*, I, 118.

passages by Swift are of the sort blamed as neurotically obscene. He wrote over three hundred poems and scores of essays. In his prose only some sections of *Gulliver* and a few other pieces are usually placed in this class; of his poems, only ten or a dozen. Properly interpreted, they would resolve themselves into either of two classes: Rabelaisian bawdy and coarseness, or – like the *Nymph going to Bed* – honest satire mixed with parody. But these critics have an easy riposte: of course, most of Swift's work is acceptable to ordinary morality; however, it is in just the few obscene passages that one meets the true Swift. Here, as Orwell says, are his 'most characteristic works'.

My reply is twofold. For one thing, it is agreed by critics, from Johnson to Huxley, that Swift was intense. He was intense when writing on politics, on religion, on economics. If he writes on prostitution, we must expect him to be intense there too. In fact, the complainants' case would be best proved if Swift were *not* intense on such subjects. Here, one might then argue, Swift shows a sudden and suspect mildness – if he did not have a neurotic fear of dung, sex, and women, he would write violently about them.

There is another answer as well. Suppose this clinching instance of Swift's ambivalent preoccupations should turn out to be not unique but a well-known motif in the popular literature of his day? One scene of *The Visions of . . . Quevedo . . . Made English by Sir R. Lestrange, and Burlesqu'd by a Person of Quality* (London, 1702) depicts a young man talking to an old man when he sees a lady of pleasure pass; she looks so fresh, young, and beautiful that he immediately tries to follow her. The old man stops him and says, in tetrameter couplets (the same form as Swift's poem):

And now I will anatomize
This creature, which inchants your eyes.
The hair she wears upon her head
Of tire-woman's borrowed;
For all her own was lost (Sir, know)
In storms which did from Naples blow.
Her eye-brows and complexion are
By skilful pencil made so fair.
All that you see of her that's good,
Continually comes from a flood
Of distill'd waters, essences,
Powders, and such like things as these,
Perfumed drawers, Spanish pockets,
Pomanders, powders, scented lockets,
All which will scarce yet qualify
The noisome poys'nous whiffs which fly
From arm-pits, toes as black as ink;
And scores of pole-cats would out-stink.
Kiss well she needs must, 'cause her lips,
(Thro' which lewd language often slips)
Are always bath'd with oyl and grease.
And if you would this thing embrace,
The better half of her you'll find
The taylor's; who, your eyes to blind,
From seeing her deformity,
With pads her body doth supply.
Take notice, when to bed she goes,
Half of her person with her shoes
She puts off, and from stinking gum
An artificial tooth doth come,
Which by her till morning lyes;
Still worser, Sir, one of her eyes
She pulls out too, that's made of glass;
Yet this must for a beauty pass![1]

[1] P. 142.

Not merely the couplets, but the scene, the images, the attitude, and many of the expressions are the same as Swift's; and the book was published during the period when he was most in London. If it be objected that only Swift would pick up such a book, enjoy it, and imitate it, the answer is that *Quevedo's Visions*, first published in a prose translation in 1667, ran through five editions within ten years. By 1715 it was in its eleventh; and it went on through the eighteenth century being happily printed and read.

Students of folklore can contribute another version of the motif, used by the Comtesse d'Aulnoy in her fairy tale, *Gracieuse and Percinet*, for the character named Duchess Grognon:

> Her hair was red as fire, her face of an alarming size, covered with pimples; she had but one blear eye left, and her mouth was so large you would have said she could eat everybody up, only, as she had no teeth, people were not afraid of it; she had a hump before and behind, and limped with both legs.

The Duchess tries to hide her ugliness from the hero:

> The ugly creature was excessively occupied with her toilette. She had one shoe made half a cubit higher in the heel than the other, in order to appear less lame, a bodice stuffed upon one shoulder to conceal the hump on its fellow. A glass eye, the best she could procure, to replace the one she had lost. She painted her brown skin white, dyed her red hair black. . . .[1]

In *Le Diable Boiteux*, Le Sage has Asmodeus show Zambullo what happens under the city roofs. In one house the watcher looks at two unpleasant sights:

[1] *Fairy Tales, by the Countess d'Aulnoy*, translated by J. R. Planché (London, 1855), pp. 1, 4.

L'un est une coquette surannée qui couche après avoir laissé ses cheveux, ses sourcils et ses dents sur sa toilette. L'autre un galant sexagénaire qui revient de faire l'amour. Il a déjà ôté son oeil et ses moustaches postiches avec sa perruque qui cachoit une tête chauve. Il attend que son valet lui ôte son bras et sa jambe de bois, pour se mettre au lit avec le reste.

In another house, he observes what looks like a beautiful, tall girl. But Asmodeus says,

Sa taille, que vous admirez, est une machine qui a épuisé les mécaniques. Sa gorge et ses hanches sont artificielles, et il n'y a pas longtemps qu'étant au sermon, elle laissa tomber ses fesses dans l'auditoire.[1]

Edgar Allan Poe's *The Man That Was Used Up* concerns a general who at first seems a most handsome person as to height, hair, whiskers, teeth, voice, eyes, chest, shoulders, and legs. At the end of the tale he is shown putting on a cork leg, a mechanical arm, false shoulders, chest pads, false teeth, a glass eye, an artificial palate and tongue, etc. Nathaniel Hawthorne's *Mrs Bullfrog*, Mark Twain's *Aurelia's Unfortunate Young Man*, and Nathanael West's *A Cool Million* employ the same device, which one scholar calls 'almost a staple motif in American humorous literature'.[2]

IV

I suggest that many 'obscene' motifs picked out as Swiftian may not be unique to Swift. The Struldbruggs are a sample: the old people in *Gulliver's Travels* who cannot die but grow more and more repulsively ancient and decayed. A friendly

[1] Chapter III (Paris, 1864), p. 14.
[2] Darrel Abel, 'Le Sage's Limping Devil and Mrs Bullfrog', *Notes and Queries*, CXCVIII (April, 1953), 166.

advocate would say that Swift is making a traditional Christian attack not on the desire for immortality but on the common yearning of the aged to go on living; he is making death less frightful than incontinent senility. There are critics who would feel unconvinced, and would claim that Swift is morbidly fascinated by the details of the spectacle. What, then, would they make of the following?

> Mrs Skewton's maid appeared, according to custom, to pre-
> pare her gradually for night. At night, [the maid] should have
> been a skeleton, with dart and hour-glass, rather than a
> woman . . . for her touch was as the touch of Death. The
> painted object shriveled underneath her hand; the form col-
> lapsed, the hair dropped off, the arched dark eyebrows changed
> to scanty tufts of grey; the pale lips shrunk, the skin became
> cadaverous and loose; an old, worn, yellow, nodding woman,
> with red eyes, alone remained in Cleopatra's place, huddled
> up, like a slovenly bundle, in a greasy flannel gown.

This is a popular Victorian novelist treating the same theme as Swift – the hideousness of age clinging to a diseased life; and he is rendering the spectacle in the only suitable way, by presenting realistic details; the book is *Dombey and Son*, by Dickens.[1]

Or take this:

> *Mistaken blessing, which old age they call!*
> *'Tis a long, nasty, darksome hospital,*
> *A ropy chain of rheums; a visage rough,*
> *Deform'd, unfeatur'd, and a skin of buff;*
> *A stitch-fall'n cheek, that hangs below the jaw;*
> *Such wrinkles, as a skilful hand would draw*
> *For an old grandam ape, when, with a grace,*
> *She sits at squat, and scrubs her leathern face. . . .*

[1] Oxford Illustrated edition, p. 393.

> *Besides th'eternal drivel, that supplies*
> *The dropping beard, from nostrils, mouth, and eyes. . . .*
> *This dotard of his broken back complains,*
> *One his legs fail, and one his shoulder pains;*
> *Another is of both his eyes bereft,*
> *And envies who has one for aiming left.*
> *A fifth with trembling lips expecting stands,*
> *As in his childhood, cramm'd by others' hands;*
> *One, who at sight of supper open'd wide*
> *His jaws before, and whetted grinders tried;*
> *Now only yawns, and waits to be supplied. . . .*[1]

It is from Dryden's version of Juvenal's tenth satire. One scholar remarks: 'Of all human wishes – for power, eloquence, military glory, . . . personal beauty – Juvenal devotes the greatest space to the vanity of the desire for a ripe old age.'[2] Juvenal on the vices of women forces one to admit that Swift's language is by comparison flaccid and innocent; the same scholar writes, 'The sixth [satire – the one on women –] is incomparably the greatest of Juvenal's satires; it is a pity that prudery prevents its being more widely read.'[3]

> *To the known brothel-house she takes her way;*
> *And for a nasty room gives double pay;*
> *That room in which the rankest harlot lay.*
> *Prepar'd for fight, expectingly she lies,*
> *With heaving breasts, and with desiring eyes:*
> *Still as one drops, another takes his place,*
> *And baffled still succeeds to like disgrace.*
> *At length, when friendly darkness is expir'd,*
> *And every strumpet from her cell retir'd,*

[1] Text from G. R. Noyes' Cambridge edition (Boston, 1950), pp. 351-2, lines 305-12, 320-1, 358-66.

[2] R. I. W. Westgate and P. L. MacKendrick, 'Juvenal and Swift', *Classical Journal*, XXXVII (1942), 468-82.   [3] Westgate, p. 468.

She lags behind, and, ling'ring at the gate,
With a repining sigh submits to fate:
All filth without, and all a fire within,
Tir'd with the toil, unsated with the sin. . . .
What care our drunken dames to whom they spread?
Wine no distinction makes of tail or head:
Who, lewdly dancing at a midnight ball,
For hot eringoes and fat oysters call;
Full brimmers to their fuddled noses thrust,
Brimmers, the last provocatives of lust;
When vapours to their swimming brains advance,
And double tapers on the tables dance.[1]

Swift's writing is sometimes coarse or bawdy, and often comic; it is usually intense, ironical, and satiric. He treats conventional themes for satire in a powerful and original style. If he succeeds more brilliantly than others, let us praise or analyse his talents. If we are shocked, let us admit it is traditions that shock us, not the man. Swift's individuality, his uniqueness and genius, do not reside in his subject-matter or in his neurosis. If we describe him as compulsive, what understanding have we gained of his art? Innumerable mortals are obsessional. Innumerable books have passages condemned as obscene. Innumerable poets have satirized women's vices, have used bold imagery, have disturbed fashionable critics. To attach these marks to Swift as damning him, and to look no further, is not to illuminate his work but to hide it.

[1] Text from Noyes, pp. 337, 340-1, lines 173-85, 416-23.

Chapter Three

LITTLE LANGUAGE

In his *Journal to Stella* Swift sometimes used a special vocabulary of more than a hundred English words, slightly distorted, which he called a 'little language'. Since John Forster in 1875 printed as much of it as he could make out from the extant manuscripts of the *Journal*,[1] commentators on the little language have brought up four problems, two of which are insoluble: the text, its literal meaning, its function, and its origin.

No remarks on the history of the little language before Swift wrote it down can be more than speculative, for neither Swift nor Stella nor Mrs Dingley has left any statement on the question; and the internal evidence is not conclusive. Yet dozens of writers have taken for granted the same improbable notion: that Esther Johnson's speech as a child was the source. This assumption may date from Forster's suggestion that Swift and she occasionally talked with one another in the little language from the time they became acquainted at Sir William Temple's.[2] Although the hypothesis cannot be proved or disproved, Margaret L. Woods – as well as Mario M. Rossi and Joseph M. Hone – has observed that since the girl was already eight years old

[1] *The Life of Jonathan Swift* (London, 1875), pp. 425-73.
[2] Forster, pp. 306-7.

when they first met, and 'by no means an idiot', she probably did not have so distorted a speech.[1]

At the function of this code, too, one can only guess. Most scholars consider it to have been for Stella an expression of Swift's tenderness toward her and of their intimacy. To Swift, Virginia Woolf wrote, it served as a refuge and an emotional release from the high formality of his social routine.[2] It was also, according to Herbert Davis, an escape from the strains of his political career.[3] These interpretations seem likely but are not susceptible of proof. More fanciful is Rossi and Hone's argument that through the little language Swift symbolically erased the age difference between Stella and himself.[4]

The basic problems of text and literal meaning have received careful treatment in the recent researches of five scholars, each one refining on his predecessors. At the end of his biography of Swift (1875), John Forster published for the first time, as accurately as he could transcribe them, all the passages of the *Journal* which were written in the little language, explaining those phrases which he thought required translation. In the first scholarly edition of the *Journal* (1897), Frederick Ryland improved on many of Forster's transcriptions, corrected some of his interpretations, noticed the 'l-r' and 'd-g' interchanges, and discussed the meaning of the two vexing 'little' words, 'richar' and 'lele'.[5] George A. Aitken founded his edition (1901) on a collation

---

[1] Margaret L. Woods, 'Swift, Stella, and Vanessa', *The Nineteenth Century*, LXXIV (December, 1913), p. 1232; Mario M. Rossi and Joseph M. Hone, *Swift or the Egotist* (New York, 1934), p. 399.
[2] 'Swift's "Journal to Stella"', in *The Second Common Reader* (New York, 1932), p. 68. [3] *Stella*, p. 86. [4] Pp. 241-2.
[5] Pp. xviii-xxi. Deane Swift, in his edition of 1768, had mentioned the 'l-r' substitution under 9 February 1710-11.

of Forster's and Ryland's readings with his own, and made additional corrections of text and translation. J. K. Moorhead continued the same process of fresh transcription and thorough collation for the Everyman volume of 1924, making still further discoveries and revisions; this was in 1948 superseded by Sir Harold Williams' definitive Clarendon edition. While preparing his volumes, Williams studied the differences between John Hawkesworth's and Deane Swift's treatments of the little language. (They were the earliest editors of the *Journal*, and the manuscripts of the portion published by Deane Swift, almost two-thirds of the whole, have been lost.) He concludes that the latter was the more faithful to the manuscripts.[1]

A systematic study of the cryptic vocabulary is still necessary, however, to correct several errors already made in interpreting it, to decipher the few words which remain uncertain in meaning, and to set forth the fairly consistent underlying code. That code is confined to those obvious examples of 'baby talk' which editors of the *Journal* have agreed in classifying as the little language and which have been satisfactorily translated.[2] Swift generally formed these specimens either by replacing a letter or two of a word by another letter, or by omitting a letter: 'love' becomes 'rove' through the substitution of 'r' for 'l'; 'hold' becomes 'hod' through the omission of 'l'. Unlike many modern codes, Swift's changes are based not on spelling but on sound; for example, any 'k' sound – be it spelled 'k', 'ck', 'ch', or 'c' – may be replaced by 't'.

[1] 'Deane Swift, Hawkesworth, and *The Journal to Stella*', in *Essays on the Eighteenth Century Presented to David Nichol Smith* (Oxford, 1945), pp. 33-48.

[2] I have taken specimens only from those letters which were printed without expurgation from the original manuscripts: numbers 1, 41-53, 55-65.

The rarest distortion is mere reduplication: 'sick' becoming 'kick' is perhaps the only pure example. Slightly more common but never, it seems, occurring alone, is the reversal of sounds: 'pocket' into 'pottick' occurs no less than twice, and at least five other words are treated in the same way. Very often one of the following letters may be omitted from a word: the 'h' of an 'sh' combination; initial or medial 'l'; medial or terminal 'r'; initial 'w'; and initial 'y'. Thus 'shall' is often written 'sall'.

By far the most frequent distortion, either alone or in combination with one of the three already mentioned, is the fairly regular substitution of certain consonantal sounds for one another. Each of the following may be found at least the number of times noted in the parentheses: 'd' for 'th' (2) or for hard 'g' (6); 'g' for 'd' (2) or for 'l' (1); 'h' for 'w' (1); 'k' or 'ck' for 't' (4); 'l' for 'r' (45); 'm' for voiced 's' (2); 'n' for 'm' (2); 'r' for 'l' (21), for 'd' (1), or for 'u' (1); 's' for 'th' (6); 't' for 'th' (1) or for 'k', 'ck', 'ch', or 'c' (13); 'z' for voiced 'th' (7) or for soft 'g' (2). These estimates take no account of repetitions of the same specimen; while 'deelest' for 'dearest' occurs scores of times, it is counted only once. Similarly, words of unclear meaning are left out of the calculations.

After making such substitutions, Swift often reverses the expected order of the letters. In 'flogive', for example, he has replaced the 'r' of 'forgive' by an 'l' and then transposed the 'l' and the 'o'. In 'flodive' he has made the further substitution of 'd' for 'g'. He also combines other techniques. Substitution of 'l' for 'r', and omission of 'y' make 'years' into 'eels'. Substitution or reduplication turns 'good' into 'dood'.

Some phrases are startling demonstrations of how the system works. 'O Rold hot a Cruttle', Swift exclaims in the entry for 21 March 1711-12, meaning, 'O Lord, what a clutter,' under the camouflage of substitution, reversal, and omission. On 10 May 1712, after reproaching Esther Johnson for not writing about her health he grants her forgiveness 'tause see im a dood dallar in odle sings' – ''cause she is a good girl in other things'. Here he has used substitution, omission, reversal, and reduplication.

These facts substantiate Moorhead's conjecture (pp. xxiv, 336n) that 'richar' means 'little' and Sir Walter Scott's frequent use of the same translation. With two exceptions 'r' regularly replaces 'l' in twenty-one or more different words – a count far higher than that for any other substitution but the complementary and unvarying 'l' for 'r'. The two exceptions are 'gangridge' ('language'), which Swift uses only once[1]; and 'maram' ('Madam'), a common word in the little language.

The most frequent mutual substitution after 'l' and 'r' is 't' and 'k' ('ck', 'ch', 'c') for one another. Although there is no example besides 'richar' of 'ch' replacing 't', there is one of 't' replacing 'ch'; 'Tlismas' for 'Christmas'. Furthermore, there are two replacements of 't' by 'ck' and many replacements of 'c' (sounded 'k') by 't'.

After these substitutions of 'l' for 'r' and 't' for 'ch' have been made, 'richar' turns into 'lital', which certainly stands for 'little' in such phrases as 'our little language' ('ourrichar Gangridge') and 'dearest little MD' ('deelest richar MD').

'Lele' is a more obscure word than 'richar'. Some suggested translations are 'truly', 'lazy', 'there', 'beloved'. The

[1] 11 March 1711-12.

code offers no easy solution of this problem. Swift may have replaced the 'r' in 'there' by 'l' and then reduplicated from 'thele' to 'lele'. But this construction is uncertain at best. Yet several contexts in which the word is used suggest that 'lele' must mean 'here' or 'there' rather often. The most convincing of these is 'lele's fol oo now, and lele's fol ee Rettle'[1] – 'there's for you now, and there's for your letter'. Deane Swift printed a significant sample – perhaps not very accurately; 'and zoo must cly Lele and Hele, and Hele aden. . . . And so leles fol ee rettle' – 'and you must cry, There and Here, and Here again. . . . And so there's for your letter.'[2] Elsewhere, Deane Swift specifically translates the word as 'there'.[3]

But this translation is meaningless in some places where 'dear' would be adequate. Swift often uses 'dee', 'deel', or 'deelest' ('dear', 'dearest') immediately before 'sollahs' ('sirrahs') or 'logues' ('rogues') as a modifier. The only other word that ever appears to be used in this position is 'lele'. A combination which also appears often is 'sollahs bose' or 'logues bose' – with slight variations; these are never preceded by any modifier except 'dee', etc., or 'lele'. Here 'lele' would be senseless as 'there' or 'here' but probably means the same as 'dee': 'dear sirrahs both' or 'dear rogues both'.

Possibly Swift was used to hearing 'dear' and 'there' so pronounced as to sound the same. His eighteenth-century biographer, Sheridan, attacked the Irish errors of pronouncing 'd' as 'th', and 'ea' invariably as 'ay'.[4] Swift, himself, in poems of the *Journal* period rhymed 'arrears' with 'repairs'

[1] 17 July 1712.   [2] 7 March 1710-11.
[3] 24 February 1710-11 (morning); 10 March 1710-11.
[4] Thomas Sheridan, *A Complete Dictionary of the English Language* (6th ed. Philadelphia, 1796), pp. 12, 54.

and 'affairs' with 'ears'; he also used many similar rhymes, as did Pope.[1] According to H. C. Wyld, all these rhymes were good at the time; i.e., the pairs of words 'might be pronounced so as to rhyme, without eccentricity, or departure from a current usage'.[2] Among people whom Swift knew, both 'there' and 'dear' may have been pronounced something like 'dhair', and he may on that account have used the same 'little' word for both of them.

Such an interpretation of one symbol by two different meanings might seem a doubtful procedure if Swift had not made similar use of 'iss' and several others of his cryptograms; once in a while he also used two 'little' words for the same English word, as both 'ickle' and 'richar' for 'little'. No internal evidence militates against the translation of 'lele' as both 'there' and 'dear', while the facts already adduced support it.

With some amplification these data can serve not only to reveal hidden meanings but also to correct two errors. The simpler of them belongs to the entry of 3 June 1711, preserved only in Deane Swift's transcription. Swift pretends to scold Stella for forgetting a name, and adds, 'Figgarkick, Soley.' Aitken suggests – and Moorhead and Williams agree – that 'Soley' must be a form of 'sollah', or 'sirrah', which seems a thoroughly plausible reading. But they also make 'Figgarkick' into 'pilgarlick'; and here I demur. Not only would this conflict with the other transliterations, but the code supplies a more convincing sense. Taking 'g' as 'd' and 'k' as 't', we get 'fiddaltick', a transparent form of the exclamation 'fiddlestick'.

A more serious misinterpretation was proposed by Emile

[1] *Poems*, I, 174, 200.   [2] *Studies in English Rhymes* (New York, 1924), p. 66.

Pons in 1937. Discussing the original manuscripts of the *Journal to Stella*, Pons argued that in them Swift twice addressed Esther Johnson secretly as 'wife', under the code of 'rife' (heretofore taken to mean 'life').[1] One of his arguments is ostensibly phonetic: 'l'equivalence $r = v$ (w) apparaît ailleurs dans le Journal, par ex. lole = love (lole me).' Even if the example were sound, it would be irrelevant. Supposing 'w' and 'v' were equivalent in Swift's code, and supposing 'lole' meant 'love', Pons would still have shown only that Swift had substituted 'l' for 'w', a possibility which has no bearing upon the problem of whether or not he substituted 'r' for 'w'. However, 'v' and 'w' were *not* equivalent for Swift, since what system he has depends on sound rather than on spelling; he never interchanges 'v' and 'w'; although he often omits initial 'w' from a word in making it 'little', he never omits 'v' – and he does manipulate several words which contain 'v'. The meaning of 'lole' is not at all certain to be 'love'; it is rare in the *Journal* and may be a wrong reading of 'lele'. Finally, while the substitution of 'l' for 'r' occurs in more than twice as many words as any other substitution, 'l' is never substituted for any additional letter – unless Pons is correct here.

Pons does not consider the facts which close the question. First, phonetically, if Swift wrote 'rife' for 'wife', it was the only occasion on which he used 'r' for 'w'. He often omits 'w'; at least once he uses 'h' for it.[2] But he never substitutes 'r'. (Of course, he almost regularly replaces 'l' by 'r', as has already been pointed out.) 'Rife' for 'wife', then, would be an extraordinary anomaly.

[1] 'Du nouveau sur le "Journal à Stella",' *Etudes anglaises*, I (May, 1937), 210-29.
[2] 12 December 1712, 'high' for 'why'.

Finally, Pons is quite wrong in asserting that 'rife' appears only twice in the *Journal to Stella* (one of these occurrences is his own discovery in a re-examination of the manuscripts). He has missed other appearances. Under 31 May 1712, Swift writes, 'farwell deelest Rives', or 'farewell, dearest lives'. Under 3 January 1712-13, he urges his two friends to 'be melly dee sollahs, & rove pdfr who roves MD bettle zan his Rife' – 'be merry, dear sirrahs, and love pdfr, who loves MD better than his life'. Precisely the same phrase occurs earlier in a letter which is not available in manuscript but the closing of which Deane Swift prints as 'love poor Presto that loves MD better than his life'.[1] Thus in an unequivocal context the prized word is undeniably intended to mean 'life'. Pons is wrong in the basis of his ingenious analysis. The 'little language' remains what it always has been: not a unique insight into Swift's passion, but a sidelight on a great man's character.

[1] 14 April 1711.

Chapter Four

HISTORY

I

All Swift's works, especially his journalism and correspondence, possess unusual interest as primary sources for historians. But his contribution to history in a formal sense is small. He composed only one finished piece of historical writing, his *Four Last Years of the Queen*, which is mainly a record of the negotiations leading to the Treaty of Utrecht; and it amounts to a defence of that treaty in very much the same way as the *Conduct of the Allies* was an attack on the preceding war. Swift has also left two fragments on Roman and medieval England, one dealing with the period before the Conquest and the other with the reigns of the four successors to William I. These fragments may belong to the years shortly before or after 1700, when Swift was little over thirty. Early in the reign of George I he wrote two semi-private memoirs or historical essays on the ministry of Oxford and Bolingbroke: *Memoirs of that Change Which Took Place in the Queen's Ministry in the Year 1710* and *An Enquiry into the Behavior of the Queen's Last Ministry*. I should also like to mark off from the rest of Swift's letters those known as the *Journal to Stella*, written almost daily from 1710 to 1713: these epistolary diaries are, for historians, the most useful of his works.

Much of this accumulation has been used in studies of the early eighteenth century by scholars of the last two hundred years, or from James Macpherson to Dr J. H. Plumb. Yet the principle of selection by which Swift decided what to put down and what to omit has hardly been considered. Lord Chesterfield said that the *Four Last Years* 'consisted chiefly of the lies of the day, which [the ministry] had in seeming confidence communicated to the Dean . . . and which the Dean took as authentic materials for history'.[1] If this was so, we may legitimately wonder exactly how so brilliant and sophisticated a propagandist could be continually hoodwinked. Besides, if Chesterfield was correct (and he gave Bolingbroke as his authority), we may ask how such eminent historians as Dr Plumb, Professor Robert Walcott, Sir Winston Churchill, and the Master of Trinity College, Cambridge, could bring themselves to use Swift's information as the source of particular facts.

It may be a help to literary and historical scholars to see what assumptions lay behind Swift's materials, since we can hardly avoid employing those materials. I shall therefore try first to analyse the preconceptions with which Swift studied all English history; and then to show how these affected his version of the period 1710-14, on which his authority is most often quoted.

That Swift should have had ambitions to write great historical works need not surprise one. The span of his life was almost coterminous with what D. C. Douglas has called 'the most prolific movement of historical scholarship which this country has ever seen'.[2] Not in England alone but in France

---

[1] Letter of 11 May 1758, to George Faulkner.
[2] *English Scholars* (London, 1939), p. 13.

and elsewhere the prestige of such studies had climbed dizzily during the seventeenth century, as statesmen, lawyers, and ecclesiastics required support in dynastic and sectarian struggles. 'The controversialists of the Middle Ages appealed to principle, their successors to history.'[1]

Besides sharing the common appreciation, Swift also made friends of several distinguished participants in this movement: Andrew Fountaine, the numismatist; other great collectors like the eighth Earl of Pembroke and the second Earl of Oxford; scholars like Thomas Carte, the biographer of Ormonde; and contemporary historians like Bishop Burnet (whom he came to detest). He had affiliations with the non-jurors, who produced the most substantial of all historical researches during the era.

In general, such men, and Swift with them, believed that the study of what Bacon called 'civil history'[2] served commonly for political and moral instruction; and in a more limited or direct way, they and their successors also 'looked to the past for prefigurations, for symbols, of contemporary events or personalities'.[3] For example, Sir William Temple, in his account of William the Conqueror, was clearly defending William of Orange.

So Swift, writing on King Stephen, keeps in mind the events leading to and following the Revolution. In summarizing the early part of Stephen's reign, Swift elaborates the parallels with William III: the succession problem, the contractual element in the king's election, Stephen's preoccupation with wars, his advancing of newcomers and giving them lands and honours, his difficulties with a pretender

[1] G. P. Gooch, *History and Historians in the Nineteenth Century* (London, 1952), p. 3. [2] *Works* (London, 1857), III, 329, 333.
[3] Pieter Geyl, *Use and Abuse of History* (New Haven, 1955), p. 12.

(Empress Maud), and his placing a foreigner (like Bentinck) at the head of his councils and army. In handling the later part of the reign, Swift draws covert analogies with James II: he treats Henry Fitz-Empress as the Prince of Orange; he describes the co-operation of the French king and the English king against Henry; he relates Stephen's vain effort to guarantee his own son's succession; and he emphasizes the bishops' refusal to comply with Stephen. Swift represents Duke William, Stephen's son, in terms of the Duke of Monmouth, and sketches William's conspiracy in terms of the Rye House Plot.[1] This sort of half-deliberate foreshadowing or hindsight is, in England, at least as old as the Tudor historians.

However, there are certain respects in which Swift, without being original, has an unusual emphasis. One relates to his view of causation. It is a truism that medieval historians normally referred causes directly to God, leaving human motivations, social pressures, or natural factors largely unexplored. With Machiavelli, Bodin, and Bacon, the intermediate causes, mainly human motives, took on great significance. 'Instead of discussing what princes ought to do in moral terms, [they] sought to understand what they did in fact, how and why they did it.'[2] Yet for Bolingbroke and the rationalists following him, the whole problem of causation (except in recent centuries) grew less interesting as earlier periods came to seem records of human folly, prejudice, ignorance, and superstition.

---

[1] Mr Myrddin Jones has explained many of these parallels in *Swift's View of History*, an unpublished B.Litt. thesis to which, in the present chapter, I am repeatedly indebted (Oxford, 1953, copy in the Bodleian Library).

[2] S. L. Goldberg, 'Sir John Hayward', *Review of English Studies*, new series, VI (1955), 234.

While Swift thoroughly appreciated the power of economic and social changes on English life within his own memory, history to him meant political history. To geography and climate he sometimes allowed a critical importance; and though generally treating wars as instruments or symptoms, he did describe them as sources for their most obvious and general effects. Normally, however, he thought that human events depended upon human hopes and fears; like most seventeenth-century historians, he looked upon history as a study of men. Thus, in handling Norman times, he shows supreme concern with the characters and deeds of the monarchs and of the chief nobles or churchmen. At the end of each reign he places a detailed portrait of the deceased king: his appearance, his ambitions, his weaknesses and vices, his talents and virtues. Swift analyses and judges him. Through the course of his narrative too, he posts psychological and ethical guides.

The determining aspects of events belonged for Swift to morality, psychology, and traditional wisdom or maxims. He assumed (as all historians must do to some extent) that the essential ingredients of human nature persist independently of time and geography: desires and anxieties are turned in different directions by different conditions, but they remain the same desires and anxieties. Otherwise, there could be nothing to tell the history *of*. So, to explain why William II failed to keep promises made during illness, Swift writes: 'It is the disposition of men who derive their vices from their complexions, that their passions usually beat strong and weak with their pulses.'[1]

To understand the course of events, therefore, one must

---

[1] *Prose Works*, ed. T. Scott (London, 1897-1908), X, 206.

understand the passions which control them. And this understanding helps to guide one's political and historical judgments. In choosing sides, however, one selects not the men with the most moderate passions but those whose interests tie them to the national welfare. By separating this welfare from the morality of its adherents, Swift could combine a dark view of human beings with a reformer's attitude toward politics. The same passions rule all parties: so he will take the party which can satisfy its passions by making the nation prosperous.

For many reasons, Swift inclined toward a deep split between appearance and actuality in his analysis of historical incidents. He felt obsessed by a doctrine which Bacon states in milder terms than he: that God 'doth hang the greatest weight upon the smallest wires, *maxima e minimis suspendens*'.[1] Swift loved to dwell on the mighty consequences of tiny events. For example, in his account of the reign of Henry I, he mentions a little wound received by Prince William, son of Duke Robert of Normandy and grandson of the Conqueror:

> [He] received a wound in his wrist, which, by the unskilfulness of a surgeon, cost him his life.
>
> This one slight inconsiderable accident did, in all probability, put a stop to very great events; for if that young prince had survived his victory, it is hardly to be doubted but through the justness of his cause, the reputation of his valour, and the assistance of the King of France, he would in a little time have recovered Normandy, and perhaps his father's liberty, which were the two designs he had in agitation; nor could he well have missed the crown of England after the King's death.[2]

[1] Bacon's *Works*, III, 334.
[2] *Prose Works*, ed. T. Scott, X, 234. Another fine example here is the account of Bishop Roger, pp. 247-8.

A correlative aspect of Swift's attitude is a preoccupation with the power of small intrigues on political history, a preoccupation which Swift deeply enjoyed. But though this notion certainly gave him vast satisfaction, it (again) was no novelty. Among those requirements for a historian which Bacon and Hobbes had learned from Machiavelli and Guicciardini was skill in unravelling intrigues.[1] Perhaps the surest reason for Swift's adopting this principle as it came down, is that it suited so many of the political events of his youth. From 1658 to 1688 intrigues lay behind some of the most considerable national decisions and crises. The Restoration, the Treaty of Dover, the Popish Plot, the Revolution, all hinged on secret transactions which might be guided by a glittering assortment of whims and passions; open proceedings again and again seemed only a cloak for hidden trivia.

Even if Swift had not learned this lesson from facts, he would have learned it from his master, Sir William Temple, whose memoirs are a record of public spirit defeated by private greed. In a verse portrait of Temple addressed to the man himself, Swift says,

> Methinks, when you expose the scene . . .
> Off fly the vizards and discover all,
> How plain I see thro' the deceit!
> How shallow! and how gross the cheat! . . .
> On what poor engines move
> The thoughts of monarchs, and designs of states,
> What petty motives rule their fates![2]

Temple, in the introduction to his own *Memoirs*, makes much of this attitude:

[1] Goldberg, p. 234.   [2] *Ode to Sir William Temple*, stanza vii.

The confidence of the king, my master, and of his chief ministers, as well as that of others abroad, gave me the advantage to discern and observe the true springs and motions of both, which were often mistaken in court, and in Parliament and thereby fasten'd many suspicions, confidences, applauses, reproaches, upon persons, and at times where they were very undeserved.[1]

However, Temple also taught Swift to believe that an ideal statesman can accomplish the greatest designs without involving himself in mean and tortuous relationships. His own reputation as a diplomat had candour as its main ingredient; and he remarks of his retirement from public life,

> I found, the arts of a court were contrary to the franckness and openness of my nature. . . . I could not talk a language I did not mean, nor serve a turn I did not like. . . . Besides, I have had in twenty years experience, enough of the uncertainty of princes, the caprices of fortune, the corruption of ministers, the violence of factions, the unsteddyness of counsels, and the infidelity of friends.[2]

If this lesson can be compounded with the other, the political philosophy which results means that while ordinary courtiers operate by intrigues and underhand schemes, a leader whom one admires must be free from such habits. So Swift, when he in turn had withdrawn from court, wrote,

> I never yet knew a minister, who was not earnestly desirous to have it thought, that the art of government was a most profound science; wheras it requires no more in reality, than diligence, honesty, and a moderate share of plain naturall sense.[3]

[1] *Memoirs* (London, 1672), sigg. A3-3ᵛ.
[2] *Memoirs, III* (London, 1709), pp. 169-71.
[3] *Prose Works*, ed. Herbert Davis (Oxford, 1939-), VIII, 139. (Cited below as Davis.)

In other words, so long as Swift followed a minister, he would have to assume that the man was frank and honest; but when he analysed the history of ordinary public events, he would assume that they sprang from obscure and devious stratagems.

The effect of this compound is to render an historian deeply vulnerable to inside information, which he will tend to trust as coming from an honest leader, no matter how sharply it conflicts with obvious facts; for the obvious cannot be the genuine cause, while the leader must be reliable. Swift's own reading added further strength to the tendency. He loved memoirs by men who 'believe themselves to have special information about hidden forces that direct the main current of events'[1]; and he considered them a special province of the French.[2] During his youth, he could read La Rochefoucauld, Villeroy, Bussy Rabutin, and others. And besides supplying him with illustrations of his doctrine, the French provided a psychology to explain it. In Montaigne, La Bruyère, and La Rochefoucauld, Swift had ready to hand the sceptical description of human pride and selfishness which perfectly matched his philosophy of history. The last source for this taste must rest in Swift's own character; yet he had to go outside himself to feed it. 'Les moindres circonstances,' says La Rochefoucauld, 'ont d'ordinaire trop de part aux plus importantes affaires.'[3] And La Bruyère, for instance, writing *De la cour*, *Des grands*, or *Du souverain*, presents rough parallels to the aphorisms with which Swift seasons his historical essays. 'Il y a peu de règles générales et de mesures certaines pour bien gouverner,' says

---

[1] D. Nichol Smith, *Characters* (Oxford, 1920), p. xxv.

[2] See his preface to Temple's *Memoirs, III.*

[3] *Mémoires*, ed. Pléiade (Paris, 1935), p. 168.

La Bruyère; 'l'on suit le temps et les conjonctures, et cela roule sur la prudence . . .' (*Du souverain*, no. 32). In the *Four Last Years*, Swift says his favourite minister thinks it 'a more easy and safe rule in politicks to watch incidents as they come, and then turn them to the advantage of what he pursues, than pretend to foresee them at a great distance'.[1]

We need not explore in detail the pessimistic formulations which Swift shared with such thinkers and which he found reinforced by them. But he unfortunately lacked the early experience of court affairs which had brought them to this tired wisdom. Here was his danger. Through the concrete tests of political business, one man may enlarge and refine his moral values so that honesty, for example, comes to seem a very intricate principle, and he learns to recognize it from the inside, under apparent deceit; or he learns to distinguish silent heroism from a bravado put on for propaganda. But another man may, to the same occupations, bring a predetermined, yardstick form of honesty and heroism, by which he approves and condemns actions seen from the outside. If the latter sort also expects crookedness from others, and yet demands a rigid integrity from himself and his leaders, he can hardly help assuming that success means deceit; and this is a mistake commonly made by inexperienced reformers. Martyrdom then becomes the final proof of a great minister: honest men are too good to succeed; they must be failures because power normally goes to the intriguers.

An illustration of the attitude appears in a defence of Sir William Temple, written either by Temple or under his direction; the author says,

[1] Davis, VII, 73.

Sir W[illiam] T[emple] no where pretends in his Memoirs
that he knew the bottom of all the court-intrigues, that were
managed with so much artifice by the prevailing ministry of
those times; nay he congratulates his good fortune that he was
never made acquainted with them; and though from several
remarkable circumstances he has all the reason imaginable to
suspect that some things were not so fairly meant as was
openly pretended, yet he knows no reason why they should
not trust him in any occasions wherein the honour of his
master or the true interest of the kingdom were concerned:
And as for the rest, he thinks it the highest complement [*sic*]
the ministry ever made him, not to disclose them to him.[1]

Swift indicates that his own ideals had this tendency when
he selects, as the heroes of all history, six figures of which
four are either suicides or martyrs: Socrates, Cato, Brutus,
and Sir Thomas More.[2] His praise of Robert, Earl of
Gloucester, in the reign of King Stephen, is another example[3]; and in the triumph of his own beloved Earl of
Oxford, Swift said, 'This man has grown by persecutions,
turnings out, and stabbing.'[4] What seems to be suggested is
almost a tragic pattern. The patriot sets forth to save his
people; the government, normally a band of scheming
intriguers, cannot resist his wisdom and integrity; he gains
control and has a sublime period of power used benevolently;
but the villains combine against him; and after serving the
country magnificently, he goes down to a defeat which not
only is more glorious than his victory, but vindicates it.

The more trivial the intrigue which brings down the
hero, the more dramatic will be the lesson of his fall. So at
the peripety of his historical myth, Swift would dwell on

[1] *Answer to . . . Monsieur de Cros*, 1693.
[2] *Gulliver*, p. 180.
[3] *Prose Works*, ed. T. Scott, X, 256.
[4] *Journal*, 22 May 1711.

the doctrine of *maxima e minimis*. Sometimes we can watch him analysing twice what he considers a cause of evil to the side which he supports: first when that side seems triumphant and second when it seems ruined. By comparing both estimates, one may observe how he enhances the triviality of a cause after it has become effective. A revealing case is that of Robethon, an agent employed by the court of Hanover. Robethon's main duty, before the death of Queen Anne, was to manage the arrangements for the Elector's succession to the British throne. In 1713, when Oxford still headed the government, Swift wrote,

> There was likewise at the Elector's court a little Frenchman without any merit or consequence called Robithon, who by the assistance and encouragement of the last ministry had insinuated himself into some degree of that prince's favour, which he used in giving his master the worst impressions he was able of those whom the Queen employed in her service.[1]

But four years later, when the Tory position looked hopeless, Swift went further. Discussing the Oxford ministry's endeavours to maintain good relations with Hanover, he wrote,

> But all endeavours were rendred abortive by a foolish circumstance which hath often made me remember the common observation of the greatest events depending frequently upon the lowest, vilest, and obscurest causes; and this is never more verified than in courts, and the issues of publick affairs. . . . It may suffice to hint at present, that a delay in conveying a very inconsiderable sum, to a very inconsiderable French vagrant, gave the opportunity to a more industrious party, of corrupting that channel through which all the idea's of the dispositions and designs of the Queen, the ministers, and the whole British nation were conveyed.[2]

[1] Davis, VII, 143-4.　　　　[2] Davis, VIII, 171-2.

Sir William Temple and the Earl of Clarendon, as portrayed by themselves, seemed like two victims of the same process. In addition, however, they stood for an element of the good historian as conceived by Swift: first-hand participation in public affairs or (a poor substitute) very close study of them. 'There was never yet a good history written', said Clarendon, 'but by men conversant in business, and of the best and most liberal education.'[1] This is an old tradition and a natural corollary of the belief that it is the function of history to make politicians wise. 'Political experience, or at least political study was regarded by . . . Bodin, Bacon, Daniel, [and] Fulke Greville . . . as an indispensable qualification for the highest form of history.'[2] In the *Journal to Stella*, written during his years of power and to his dearest friend, Swift has hints of foreseeing the value of the confidences which he sends her: 'This will be a memorable letter', he once wrote, 'and I shall sigh to see it some years hence.' 'My letters would be good memoirs', he writes another time, 'if I durst venture to say a thousand things that pass.'[3] A sophist might even suggest that one reason Swift took up pamphleteering was, by working with a ministry, to train himself to write a great historical composition.

That this was not wholly absent from his motives appears in his ambition to be made Historiographer Royal. The office carried a small (though not negligible) salary, and Swift hankered after it before he even met Robert Harley or Henry St John. During the years 1710-14, when he felt intimate with the heads of the state, he repeatedly angled for the historiographer's place; and during the general col-

[1] *Collection of Several Tracts* (London, 1727), pp. 80-81.
[2] Goldberg, p. 234.   [3] 15 December 1711; 14 March 1712-13.

lapse of his friends' government in the summer of 1714, this remained among Swift's boldest desiderata.

II

What Swift – though not all his readers – overlooked, was the chance that he might himself become the instrument of others. And even his most critical readers have (I think) not noticed that he did act in effect as the spokesman of one person above all. Swift liked to feel that his pamphlets expressed his own beliefs; and though he looked for a solid preferment, he refused any intermediate reward. All his productions in support of Oxford's ministry brought him no payment in cash, since he would accept none. He felt satisfied to possess the friendship of great men as an acknowledgement of his genius, and to preserve his independence of them except in the matter of an ultimate bishopric or deanery. Swift could tell himself as well as others that he lay under no obligation to the government whose policies he chose to defend, that while his arguments had the advantage of confidential information, his opinions were wholly his own, unwarped and impartial.

Although such a man would not be controlled through bribes or a salary, he might be managed through conversations, hospitality, friendship, and (most subtly) control of the data which he was given. A brilliant prose style is not enough to make political pamphlets effective. Swift needed facts which the opposition writers lacked. Having access to the lord treasurer and the secretary of state, he could easily acquire such knowledge. But he would not acquire the same set of facts from both. Oxford and Bolingbroke were engaged in a feud from the time they came to power. The secretary schemed to replace the treasurer, and the treasurer acted so as to block the secretary.

At first Swift fell into the error of supposing they were friends. Later, he discovered they were not; but he mistakenly thought that their enmity had an essentially personal foundation, that they supported the same programme. In the end, he still attributed Oxford's evasiveness to defects of character rather than to his obscure pursuit of a policy with which Bolingbroke avowedly disagreed. Because of these errors, Swift worked for Bolingbroke much more than for Oxford, and yet conceived of himself as the partisan of neither. He was not, however, 'captured' by the secretary, because he really believed in Bolingbroke's principles (regardless of the sincerity with which they were put forward).

Oxford and Bolingbroke both had wished to end the war with France, to maintain the Hanoverian succession, and to keep the Whig Junto out of the government; they clashed in that they both also wanted supreme power. Oxford hoped furthermore, to stay in office by juggling the opposition and the high church extremists against one another. Bolingbroke fought him by a thoroughgoing strategy aimed at crushing the nonconformists and throwing all power to the country party and the high church men. Swift saw through his own earliest impressions of the ministers, but he continued to judge that the opposition were a menace to the constitution. Since he believed that one should support leaders whose 'safety and interest are visibly united with those of the publick',[1] he did not stop defending his friends, in spite of

[1] Davis, VIII, 85.

their private ambitions. But when, in May 1714, having retired from court, he quite frankly and honestly offered a scheme of his own, it was a thoroughgoing programme: dissenters not to be 'trusted with the smallest degree of civil or military power' and the 'Whigs, low-church, republicans, moderation-men, and the like, [to] receive no marks of favour from the crown, but what they should deserve by a sincere reformation'.[1]

Even if Swift had not happened to sympathize more with Bolingbroke's views than with Oxford's, there were indirect lures to attract him; for these two men had very different ways of handling people. Oxford rarely made his plans clear; he expected any collaborator to pick up clues, to sense what would please him, and to act without explicit instructions. The real freedom to make decisions, he kept to himself, often taking important new steps which his colleagues did not anticipate. One of his most critical measures, to create twelve new peers, seems to have been concerted entirely between the queen and himself. All accounts agree that Oxford was a secretive and vague procrastinator. Swift often speaks of seeing him, rarely of obtaining valuable data from him. 'I dined with lord treasurer,' he says in July 1711, 'but cannot get him to do his own business with me; he has put me off.'[2] Six months later, he says, 'Lord treasurer gave me [some papers] last night, as he always does, too late.'[3]

Oxford's methods can be inferred from his treatment of Daniel Defoe. 'So far from dictating a policy . . . Harley was constantly looking around for suggestions.'[4] It was Defoe who had to guess at the minister's desires, to ask for

[1] Davis, VIII, 88. [2] *Journal*, 20 July 1711.
[3] *Journal*, 12 February 1711-12.
[4] James Sutherland, *Defoe* (London, 1937), p. 107.

approval of his own essays, to listen for cues in Oxford's conversation. 'Might I reciev the least remote hint from your Ldpp', Defoe writes to Oxford,

> Something might easily be said without doores, that would take off all the edge of the popular surprize some people think they have rais'd. . . . If your Ldpp please but to hint your commands to Mr Read [probably Oxford's porter] by a single *yes* or *no*, it is enough to be understood by me, and shall be immediately obey'd, I hope to your Ldpps satisfaction. I mean *yes* or *no* onely whether . . . [such an argument] may be usefull at this time. . . . I humbly ask your Ldpps pardon for this motion.[1]

The man who could drive Defoe to write this, was obviously not prepared to be explicit with Swift.

Bolingbroke, on the contrary, loved to talk. His strength in the House of Commons depended a great deal on his oratory. In private, he gave an appearance of speaking without premeditation, frankly, and off the record. But we may gather what calculation lay behind his manner from a remark which he made to Swift the first time they met: 'He told me . . . that Mr Harley complained he could keep nothing from me, I had the way so much of getting into him.'[2] Swift was not so naïve as to believe such flattery so early in their friendship. Yet four months later he writes ingenuously, 'Mr Harley . . . confessed to me, that uttering his mind to me gave him ease.'[3] Swift would hardly have taken the bait so soon if he had not felt eager for it. When the ministers told him that they trusted him, they said what he wished to hear. But I suspect that while they did like

[1] Letter of 27 May 1712.   [2] *Journal*, 11 November 1710.
[3] *Journal*, 4 March 1710-11.

Swift, and trusted in his honesty and good will, they knew better than to present him with any secrets which they were not willing to have him repeat.

Swift, then, was predisposed to agree with Bolingbroke; he also received far more information through him than through Oxford; and therefore we may expect his polemical activities to show a corresponding bias. While Defoe produced pamphlets to support Oxford's domestic policies, Swift's essays were largely on foreign affairs, Bolingbroke's territory. And in Swift's interpretation of contemporary history, not only can a number of dubious statements be attributed to Bolingbroke, but I think we can observe the secretary turning him against persons whom Bolingbroke feared. The treatment of the Duke of Marlborough is a good illustration. Swift's portrait of Marlborough in the *Four Last Years* is one of his most stunning jobs of character assassination:

I shall say nothing of his military accomplishments, which the opposite reports of his friends and enemies among the soldiers have rendred in some manner problematical: But, if he be among those who delight in war, it is agreed to be not for the reasons common with other generals. Those maligners who deny him personal valour, seem not to consider, that this accusation is charged at a venture; since the person of a wise general is too seldom exposed, to form any judgement in the matter: And, that fear, which is said to have sometimes disconcerted him before an action, might probably be more for his army than for himself. He was bred in the height of what is called the Tory principle; and continued with a strong biass that way, until the other party had bid higher for him than his friends could afford to give. His want of literature is in some sort supplyed by a good understanding, a degree of natural elocution, and that knowledge of the world which is learned in armies and courts. We are not to take the height of his ambition from his soliciting to be general for life: I am persuaded, his chief motive was the pay and perquisites by continuing the war; and, that he had *then* no intentions of settling the crown in his family; his only son having been dead some years before. He is noted to be master of great temper; able to govern, or very well disguise his passions, which are all melted down or extinguished in his love of wealth. That liberality which nature hath denied him with respect to money, he makes up by a great profusion of promises: But, this perfection so necessary in courts, is not very successful in camps, among soldiers who are not refined enough to understand or to relish it.[1]

The self-consciousness of Swift's artistry should not suggest that he disagreed with his own language. His attitude toward Marlborough can be traced through the *Journal to Stella*: his private expressions there are in remarkable harmony with the portrait which appears in the *Four Last Years*; and that, in turn, agrees with the number of the *Examiner* attacking Marlborough as Crassus. Yet all these representations are profoundly misleading. Swift begrudges Marlborough even his generalship, and drowns all his good parts in his avarice. Swift could do so because he was relying on inside information.

In a description of Marlborough written December 1710, Swift says,

He is covetous as Hell, and ambitious as the prince of it: he would fain have been general for life, and has broken all endeavours for peace, to keep his greatness and get money.[2]

This is preceded by Swift's remarking that he had seen

---

[1] Davis, VII, 7-8.   [2] *Journal*, 31 December 1710.

Bolingbroke that morning and that Bolingbroke said he had been with Marlborough. A year later Swift says, 'I confess my belief that [Marlborough] has not one good quality in the world besides that of a general, and even that I have heard denied by several great soldiers.' This follows the remark, 'I dined with the secretary, and it is true that the duke of Marlborough is turned out of all.' On the same occasion, Bolingbroke also dropped another insinuation as well; for he told Swift that the real cause of Marlborough's fall was not his vices but the dislike which Oxford and the Queen felt for him. The spark took; and Swift, disappointed to think that Oxford governed by whim, wrote, 'I do not love to see personal resentment mix with public affairs.'[1] A week later, we find a still balder innuendo: Swift says,

> The duke of Marlborough says, There is nothing he now desires so much as to contrive some way how to soften Dr Swift. . . . Mr secretary told me this from a friend of the duke's.[2]

Again he believed, for again there was no authority which he put before that of the secretary of state.

In these circumstances Swift could not help drifting to Bolingbroke's side; and I think several misleading facts attributed to Swift can be traced to this relationship. Sir Winston Churchill, in his life of Marlborough, quotes from the *Journal*, '[The] Queen and Lord Treasurer mortally hate the Duke of Marlborough, and to that he owes his fall.'[3] Now Swift never spoke to her majesty or his grace. But if we go to the original letter, we see, as I have just indicated, that Swift's statement came from Bolingbroke. Of course, the treasurer and the queen felt deeply reluctant to part with

[1] *Journal*, 1 January 1711-12.   [2] Ibid.   [3] London, 1947, II, 915.

Marlborough; they were compelled to do so because peace would otherwise have been impossible.

Nicholson and Turberville, in their life of the Duke of Shrewsbury, quote Swift on the Duke's conduct as lord lieutenant of Ireland. He says Shrewsbury's actions were 'directly opposite to the court'.[1] The truth is, Shrewsbury acted in direct opposition to Bolingbroke. In Ireland it was the lord chancellor, Phipps, who held the confidence of Bolingbroke's faction; but Shrewsbury had Oxford and the queen behind him. Swift, on Bolingbroke's information, naturally misconstrued the situation.

Similar fallacies occur here and there in other studies. Professor Walcott describes Swift's *Memoirs* . . . [*of*] *1710* among accounts stemming 'from Harley' himself, although the bias of the essay is due less to him than to Bolingbroke.[2] Dr Plumb calls the creation of twelve Tory peers a decision 'taken by the ministry', although it was certainly a secret from Bolingbroke.[3]

Through his fondness for psychology, moralizing, and intrigue, Swift fell a happy victim to private communications from inspired sources; and he was similarly fortified against rational, inductive arguments put forward by an opposition. When he believed both that men in power had motives which it would be impolitic for them to publish, and also that they had confidentially entrusted him with these true sources of their known conduct, he could stand out against the most direct assault from facts; for he was

[1] Davis, VIII, 156; cf. T. C. Nicholson and A. S. Turberville, *Charles Talbot, Duke of Shrewsbury* (Cambridge, 1930), p. 205. Swift knew that Shrewsbury disliked Bolingbroke; see Swift's letter of 7 August 1714, to Charles Ford.
[2] Robert Walcott, *English Politics in the Early Eighteenth Century* (Oxford, 1956), p. 154.   [3] J. H. Plumb, *Sir Robert Walpole* (London, 1956), p. 178.

always prepared to classify open pronouncements as propaganda, and to presume that the real aims were the unknown aims. If Swift had had less experience in directing the opinions of others, he might have followed safer standards in forming his own.

Nevertheless, and contrary to Chesterfield's opinion, Swift did not merely swallow lies. He supported the ministers not out of pure gullibility but from conscious principles. This attitude he never lost, and in print he refused to go back on his sentiments of 1710-12. However, less than a year after meeting Oxford and Bolingbroke, he not only realized that they were rivals but was already trying to reconcile them; for he did not yet appreciate the depth of their antipathy. During the autumn of 1713 he wrote a memorandum bluntly criticizing Oxford's policies.[1] In the spring of 1714 he withdrew from court, considering the internal situation of the ministry to be beyond repair. In May 1714 he produced *Some Free Thoughts*, criticizing mainly Oxford but also (though very slightly) Bolingbroke. The latter, he complains of as contending 'for a greater part in the direction of affairs' than belonged to him, and as carrying his resentment at Oxford's refusal 'further than private friendship or the safety of the public would admit'.[2] *Some Free Thoughts* speaks for Bolingbroke very much as Defoe's *Secret History of the White Staff*, written probably four months later, was to speak for Oxford. Expressing himself with few inhibitions and with entire honesty, Swift shows that he did not approve of Oxford's balancing projects and did not understand how far Oxford was committed to them. He did not, therefore,

[1] See the *Bulletin of the John Rylands Library*, XXXVII (March, 1955), pp. 382-4.
[2] Davis, VIII, 87.

blindly digest mendacities; but he gratefully accepted materials which seemed to confirm his own opinions. He was neither a hypocrite nor a complete dupe.

He was not objective either. His *Four Last Years* contains many errors which are due to his taking gossip seriously and his failing to check up on rumours which he wished to believe. Nevertheless, historians would be ill-advised to reject his contributions for that reason. Nobody who has committed himself to one party in a political struggle can afford to write impartially concerning that struggle. Since an unprejudiced history is not conceivable, I suggest that Swift's accomplishment, particularly the *Journal to Stella*, is of high value. In his works, scholars are fortunate to have both the records of an informed observer and the source of his bias. We can allow for his commitments on all levels, and judge through him what forces were at work behind the outward alignments.

On two issues I must defend him against traditional accusations: his honesty and his fundamental correctness in judging the events of 1708 to 1715. Although Swift often withheld information, darkened the characters of the opposition, or idealized the motives of his own side, I find no instance of his either writing against his principles or accepting doctrines without being persuaded of their soundness. There is an amazing consistency between the statements made in his pamphlets, his memoirs, his letters, and his journals. I also believe that he did not go far wrong in his broad analysis of contemporary history. The Peace of Utrecht was a great and necessary achievement; the mass of enfranchised Englishmen did oppose the Junto and did support Swift's friends. Before the Queen's death, Oxford and Bolingbroke had no more dangerous dealings with the Pretender than Godolphin, Marlborough, and Shrewsbury. George I, as Elector, did play into the hands of a faction. But not until twenty years after Swift's death did it become feasible to set the record straight. Then Macpherson's volumes on the Restoration and the reign of Queen Anne corroborated Swift (in general though not in detail). As the works of Hume, Dalrymple, and others followed, the so-called Tory interpretation of political history began to establish itself; and for the time being, Swift might have felt himself vindicated.

Chapter Five

GULLIVER

I

U ntil the publication of the *Letters to Ford*, literary scholars thought that Swift wrote *Gulliver's Travels* between 1715 and 1720, a period when he published almost nothing.[1] His starting-point was, they believed, sketches made up by the Scriblerus group – Pope, Swift, and others – in 1713 and 1714, and finally produced by Pope in 1741. Then Professor Nichol Smith, in his edition of the Ford letters, proved that Swift wrote Part I of *Gulliver* in about 1721-2, Part II around 1722-3, Part IV in 1723, and Part III (after Part IV) in 1724-5. Swift continued to revise the whole book, probably until it was published in the autumn of 1726.

But if Professor Nichol Smith's facts have long been accepted, very few implications have been drawn from them. It is still normal for critics discussing the composition of the book to begin with Scriblerus, as it is still normal for them to seek later sources in literature and in political or intellectual history.[2] If, however, the Scriblerus papers seemed a

---

[1] *The Letters of Jonathan Swift to Charles Ford*, ed. D. Nichol Smith (Oxford, 1935), pp. xxxviii-xlii. Sir Charles Firth used some of Professor Nichol Smith's evidence (not quite correctly) in 'The Political Significance of *Gulliver's Travels*', *Proceedings of the British Academy*, IX (1920), 237-59.

[2] For recent examples, see Ricardo Quintana, *Swift, an Introduction* (Oxford,

probable beginning for *Gulliver* precisely because Swift worked on them just before he composed *A Voyage to Lilliput* in 1715, surely the discovery of a six-year gap makes it less necessary to consider them. It may have seemed likely that Swift, after leaving in 1714 both England and his friends of the Scriblerus Club, should in 1715 have projected a satire based on Scriblerus essays. It is less plausible that he should have waited six or seven years before hauling out sketches theretofore unused, and employing them as the frame for his greatest book.

Nevertheless, the original argument is useful: ought one not to look at what Swift was indeed busy with, just before the genuine date of his start on *Lilliput*? For not only were the early biographers and critics mistaken as to that date; they were also wrong to suppose that, because Swift published nothing in the years preceding *Gulliver*, he wrote nothing. It was during this period that he put together a succession of essays concerning English politics mainly from 1708 to 1715. Furthermore, these essays form stages in a long series of works and fragments dealing with the same subject but none of them innocent enough to be published at the time. Finally one remembers that Part I of *Gulliver* is largely an allegory of English political history from 1708 to 1715, and that in this allegory Gulliver stands largely for Bolingbroke, the secretary of state from 1710 to 1714.

It seems to me more than a coincidence that Swift wrote essay after unprintable essay on English politics of the early eighteenth century, and then plunged into such an

1955), pp. 145ff; and Charles Kerby-Miller, ed., *Memoirs of . . . Scriblerus* (New Haven, 1950), pp. 315-20.

allegory. To ignore Swift's *History of the Four Last Years*, his *Some Free Thoughts upon the Present State of Affairs*, his *Memoirs . . . 1710*, his various fragments on the same topics, and then to search for *Gulliver's* antecedents in a vague ur-*Scriblerus* is to contradict all we have learned of his literary method. What one knows of the *Memoirs of Scriblerus* belongs almost entirely to its form in 1741, fifteen years after the printing of *Gulliver*, a form which Pope had deliberately edited so as to connect the book with Swift's masterpiece.[1] Is it credible that an author should compose hundreds of poems practically all traceable to specific circumstances, and scores of essays or pamphlets which can hardly be understood except by reference to their occasions, and yet should compose his finest work in a library, referring to old drafts of hypothetical hoaxes?

I shall not only suggest that Swift created much of *Gulliver* out of his own memories, experiences, and reflections from 1714 to 1725; but moving from this position, I shall try to indicate some new meanings for certain parts of the book.

II

Professor Arthur E. Case, refining on Sir Charles Firth, has already explained the political allusions in *A Voyage to Lilliput*; and there is not a great deal to alter in his foundations.[2] Both scholars went astray, however, in comparing *Lilliput* with the actual events of 1708 to 1715 and not with Swift's versions of those events. If Case had looked into Swift instead of history, he would have found that the

---

[1] Kerby-Miller, pp. 61-65.
[2] *Four Essays on Gulliver's Travels* (Princeton, 1945), pp. 69-80.

political allegory is both more detailed and less consistent than he believed; that references to Bolingbroke (rather than Oxford) control the fable; and that Swift tended to choose, for dramatization, those episodes in which he could identify his own feelings with those of the ministry. There are many examples of these principles, though I shall limit myself to three.

In Chapter II of *Lilliput*, although Gulliver is under a strong guard, he is unavoidably exposed to the 'impertinence' and 'malice' of the 'rabble', some of whom shoot arrows at him. But 'the Colonel' delivers six of the ringleaders into his hands. Gulliver frightens each one by pretending he will eat the man alive and then setting him free. In the *Battle of the Books*, Swift calls journalists 'a disorderly rout' of coatless 'rogues and raggamuffins'.[1] In his letters to Ford he calls Oxford 'the Colonel' and Bolingbroke 'the Captain'.[2] In the *Journal to Stella* he complains that Whig pamphleteers are busy against the government: 'I have begged [Bolingbroke] to make examples of one or two of them; and he assures me he will. They are very bold and abusive.' The following month, he says that one journalist – Boyer –

> has abused me in a pamphlet, and I have got him up in a messenger's hands: [Bolingbroke] promises me to swinge him. [Oxford] told me last night that he had the honour to be abused with me in a pamphlet. I must make that rogue an example for warning to others.

A week later, he reports that 'every day some ballad comes

---

[1] *A Tale of a Tub*, ed. D. Nichol Smith (Oxford, 1920), p. 238.

[2] For convenience, I call Oxford and Bolingbroke by their titles even before they were created peers.

out reflecting on the ministry'; and Bolingbroke 'has seized on a dozen booksellers and publishers'.[1]

It was under Bolingbroke, as secretary of state, that we first see the government trying to stamp out journalistic opposition by means of frequent arrests rather than by court action. 'Warrants were issued in large numbers. Arrests were made, and printers were required to furnish sureties for appearance.' But the government's powers did not often permit anything more serious than such harrying and frightening manoeuvres:

> And yet of these thirteen [Swift's dozen] who were seized, Boyer, who would not be likely to ignore martyrs for the Whig cause, mentions not one as suffering punishment. And in 1712 Bolingbroke was compelled to order the Attorney-General to release a number of persons under prosecution for libel.[2]

Swift, libelled like the government, has thus created an allegorical detail from Bolingbroke's method of dealing with the dart-throwing hack writers of 1710-14.

In Chapter V of *Lilliput*, there is the crisis about which Case and Firth disagreed, the fire in the palace, which Gulliver quenches with his urine. Firth supposed this to mean *A Tale of a Tub*; Case interpreted it as the Treaty of Utrecht, ending the War of the Spanish Succession. Case is undoubtedly correct. The meaning appears from a sentence in a pamphlet written by an underling in 1714 with Swift's assistance:

---

[1] 21 September, 16 October, and 24 October 1711. Four months after this last date, there was a rumour that Swift had been arrested. In an odd coincidence, he mentions this and the pamphleteers together, thus joining the themes of the episode in *Gulliver*: 'I doubt you have been in pain about the report of my being arrested. The pamphleteers have let me alone this month' (17, 18 February 1712).

[2] Laurence Hanson, *Government and the Press 1695-1763* (Oxford, 1936), p. 62.

But the quarrelling with the peace, because it is not exactly to our mind, seems as if one that had put out a great fire should be sued by the neighbourhood for some lost goods, or damag'd houses; which happen'd (say they) by his making too much haste.[1]

The figure of extinguishing a spreading blaze for stopping, by allied action, a tremendous military threat, is ancient, natural, and ubiquitous. A few scattered modern instances are found in the Emperor Maximilian's declaration against the Venetians, 1509; Samuel Daniel's *Breviary of the History of England*, ca. 1610; the Italian satirist, Boccalini, writing about the Fronde; and (most relevantly) the London *Flying-Post*, 25 October 1712, applying Boccalini to the War of the Spanish Succession:

> A dreadful fire broke out in the palace of the French monarchy. . . . It raged so furiously, that the neighbouring monarchs, afraid that their own estates would be consumed by it, immediately ran one and all to quench it. The English . . . diligently carried thither the waters of their Thames.[2]

Yet Case mistakes the implications when he relates them to Oxford's difficulties with Queen Anne.[3] It was not the queen who felt ungrateful for the peace, but those who impeached the ministers. The treaty was Bolingbroke's peculiar responsibility; and Swift's emphasis on it – as well as his preoccupation, throughout the first voyage, with foreign rather than domestic affairs – betokens Bolingbroke's predominance in the Lilliputian allegory. By 1721, after all, it was not

[1] Davis, VIII, xvi-xvii, 194.
[2] See Raynaldus, *Annales ecclesiastici*, XX (Rome, 1663), annus 1509, ¶ 2; Daniel's *Breviary*, ¶ 27; Chapter III of the 1704 translation of Boccalini's *Advertisements from Parnassus . . . [and] The Politick Touchstone*, III, 7-11 (following p. 256).
[3] Case, pp. 75-76.

Oxford who wanted defending: he had been discharged
from his impeachment in 1717; and he acted a free role in
the House of Lords until his death in 1724 – well before the
completion of *Gulliver's Travels*. Bolingbroke, meanwhile,
having fled to France in 1715, remained attainted and in
exile until 1723; and he never regained his seat in the House
of Lords.

The same inferences emerge again from my final illustration; and this will carry us to a point after which, Case himself says, Gulliver's story is based on Bolingbroke's adven-
tures, with only minor references to Oxford.[1] In Chapter V
of Part I, Swift mentions the displeasure of the Emperor of
Lilliput when Gulliver made friends with the ambassadors
from Blefuscu and agreed to visit their emperor, thus creat-
ing a suspicion of high treason: certain ministers, says
Gulliver,

> represented my intercourse with those ambassadors as a mark
> of disaffection, from which I am sure *my heart was wholly free*.[2]

Here, one already knows, Blefuscu stands for France. From
evidence in Swift's letters and pamphlets, it seems that the
proposed visit to the Emperor of Blefuscu stands for Bolingbroke's visit (while he was secretary of state) to the French
court; and the suspicion of his disaffection would be due to
Bolingbroke's having seen the Pretender during that visit.

In the *Enquiry into the Behavior of the Queen's Last Ministry*,
Swift has a portrait of Bolingbroke. Here is a pamphlet defending Swift's ministerial acquaintances against the charge
(among others) of planning to bring in the Pretender and so
to commit high treason. Swift opens the portrait of Boling-

---

[1] Case, p. 77.   [2] p. 63 (my italics).

broke with a lament that three of his most exalted friends are either in exile or awaiting trial. Then he applies to himself the same expression that Gulliver was to use:

> *As my own heart was free* from all treasonable thoughts, so I did little imagine my self to be perpetually in the company of traytors.[1]

This passage, written in 1715, has a further parallel in Swift's letter on the subject. The Archbishop of Dublin had suggested that Bolingbroke might turn informer, come back from France, and tell some 'ill story' about Swift. In reply, the Archbishop received a furious defence of the exile:

> He was three or four days at the court of France, while he was secretary, and it is barely possible, he might then have entered into some deep negotiation with the Pretender; although I would not believe him, if he should swear it, because he protested to me, that he never saw him but once, and that was at a great distance, in public, at an opera. . . . But I am surprised to think your grace could talk, or act, or correspond with me for some years past, while you must needs believe me a most false and vile man; declaring to you on all occasions my abhorrence of the Pretender, and yet privately engaged with a ministry to bring him in.[2]

Finally, returning to *Lilliput*, one finds, in Chapter VII, the fourth article of the impeachment against Gulliver – that

> contrary to the duty of a faithful subject, [he] is now preparing to make a voyage to the court and empire of Blefuscu . . . [and] doth falsely and traitorously intend to take the said voyage, and thereby to aid, comfort, and abet the Emperor of Blefuscu, so late an enemy, and in open war with his imperial majesty aforesaid.

In other words, the treason charged against Gulliver corre-

[1] Davis, VIII, 134 (my italics). [2] Ball, II, 348-9.

sponds to that against Bolingbroke, which touches Swift as well; and Gulliver's projected trip corresponds to Bolingbroke's actual trip.

These echoes and parallels hold a few of the many clues which bear out my principal argument. Swift did not wait six years after 1714 to prepare his reflections on the ministry of the Earl of Oxford and Viscount Bolingbroke. He went over the material in one form after another, from personal letters, through unpublishable essays, into the entertainment of an allegory. *Lilliput* is a sublimation of the suppressed pamphlets and fragments. The *Memoirs of Scriblerus* may have been an element in the allegory, but only an indeterminate element.[1]

Even so, one must not confound origins with value. *Lilliput* does not signify a container for private jokes or half-conscious allusions. Its theme is Pascal's 'Qu'est-ce qu'un homme dans l'infini?'[2] Regarding the pigmies from a giant's height, the reader feels how trifling are human ambitions when impartially judged. To sharpen the comedy and to focus the irony, Swift also closes the apparent distance between Gulliver and his hosts; for the traveller often glories in the errors which he condemns, revealing by turns his own vanity, chauvinism, cruelty, and arrogance. *Lilliput* is part of a satire on human pride, and the physical proportions stand for a moral ratio. In tracing a possible lineage for the central person of this parable, I have no wish to limit its meaning.

[1] Employing very different arguments, Case reaches conclusions like my own (pp. 102-6).

[2] 'Disproportion de l'homme', (*Pensées*, ed. Victor Giraud, Paris, 1928, p. 37). I quote from Pascal, here and below, because the parallels seem interesting. The ideas themselves are commonplaces, however, and there is no question of influence.

III

If the pigmies of Lilliput are dominated by a figure descended from Bolingbroke, the giants of Brobdingnag are ruled by one exactly the opposite in origin. This is the person to whom Swift immediately contrasted Bolingbroke the first time that he met the secretary. On the evening of that day, Swift wrote to Stella,

> I am thinking what a veneration we used to have for Sir William Temple, because he might have been secretary of state at fifty; and here is a young fellow, hardly thirty, in that employment.

A year later, he drew precisely the same contrast again, obviously forgetting that he had already noticed it. In fact, out of a total of seven times that Swift mentions Temple in the *Journal to Stella*, five are to link or contrast him with Bolingbroke.[1]

Indeed, between those two great men, the similarities of interest and achievement, and the differences of character, are so startling that the image of one would naturally call up an image of the other. Bolingbroke talked too much, drank too much, systematically betrayed his wife, and sacrificed his integrity to political ambition. Temple spoke with reserve and formality; he lived with calculated moderation; he adored his wife, the brilliant Dorothy Osborne; he withdrew from high office rather than injure his honour. Both men had their greatest successes in diplomacy. Temple arranged the Triple Alliance of England, Holland, and Sweden; he was largely responsible for the marriage of William of Orange to Princess Mary. Bolingbroke's supreme

[1] 11 November 1710; 3, 4, 15 April 1711; 3 November 1711.

achievement was the Treaty of Utrecht. Temple had refused at forty-six to be made secretary of state; Bolingbroke had forced his way into the office.

If Swift's memory of Temple provided the outline for the King of Brobdingnag, certain other aspects of the second voyage slip into place. I have already argued that the child Stella, or Esther Johnson, has a similar relationship to the girl giantess, Glumdalclitch; and of course Swift knew Stella as a child, while they were both living with Temple. In several aspects the Moor Park family seem tinged with regal colour. Lady Temple, or Dorothy Osborne, is naturally associated with a queen since she was the intimate friend of Queen Mary, whose death narrowly preceded her own. There is a further hint here; for in Brobdingnag the giant queen plays a far more dignified role, and has far more to do, than in any of the other courts which Gulliver visited. Yet the king remains emphatically in control of the monarchy. The reign of William and Mary duplicates this relationship, as did no other royal couple in Swift's lifetime before 1726; and that reign roughly coincides with the extent of Swift's residences at Moor Park. One might add, among Temple's links with kingship, that he bore the same name as William III, was a most esteemed friend of that ruler, and introduced Swift to him – the only king Swift met before 1726.

Gulliver's portrait of the King of Brobdingnag agrees in many essentials with the character of Temple. The giant had married a wife who, like Dorothy Osborne, possessed an 'infinite deal of wit and humour'. When Gulliver first met him, the king was 'retired to his cabinet'. Gulliver almost never describes him in society, almost always converses with him alone, and remarks that the geography of his country made him live in it 'wholly secluded from the rest of the world'. But he 'delighted in musick', was 'educated in the study of philosophy', had an 'excellent understanding', and was 'as learned as any person in his dominions'. In examining Gulliver's body, the king showed up the quackery of certain pedants who pretended to be wise men.[1]

Temple's own sister says that immediately after his marriage he had, for five years, lived a domestic and retired life, spending much time 'in his closet', studying history and philosophy. She comments on his excellent knowledge of Spanish, French, and Latin, and his regret at the decline of his Greek; and she says he was 'a great lover of musick'.[2] In the *Ode to Sir William Temple*, Swift has a stanza contrasting the baronet's polished but solid learning with the 'ill-mannered pedantry' of professional scholars.[3] During the decade when Swift stayed with Temple, the baronet's sister says her brother utterly withdrew from court and town life, living in rural seclusion with his family.[4] The King of Brobdingnag spoke at first in a cold manner and produced an impression 'of much gravity, and austere countenance'. Temple's reserve and aloofness are perhaps the best-known traits of his character, and Swift mentions them in the *Journal to Stella*.[5]

In politics, the King of Brobdingnag 'professed both to abominate and despise all *mystery*, *refinement*, and *intrigue*, either [of] a prince or a minister'.[6] In his *Ode* Swift devotes

[1] *Gulliver*, pp. 134-7, 167, 179.
[2] G. C. Moore Smith, ed. *The Early Essays and Romances of Sir William Temple* (Oxford, 1930), pp. 8, 5, 6, 11, 28.
[3] Stanza iii.   [4] Moore Smith, pp. 25, 28.
[5] *Gulliver*, pp. 134-5; *Journal*, 3-4 April 1711.   [6] *Gulliver*, p. 181.

a stanza to Temple's destructive exposure of the deceits and frauds of ministers.[1] Temple's actual conduct as a diplomat was distinguished above all for its directness and its lack of intrigue or ceremony. The giant king feels overwhelmed by horror at Gulliver's description of human warfare, and cannot understand why the British in particular have engaged in 'such chargeable and extensive wars'. Swift in his *Ode* has two stanzas on Temple's repugnance for war.[2] Summing up the king's nature, Gulliver granted him 'every quality which procures veneration, love, and esteem'. In his *Ode* Swift says that Temple is learned, good, and great all at once, and uniquely joins in himself the whole empire of virtue. When Temple died, Swift wrote, 'With him [died] all that was good and amiable among men.'[3]

The King of Brobdingnag talks about government and politics in Chapter VI of the second voyage. After hearing Gulliver explain the constitution of England, he asks many questions. Though these are satirical, they involve certain arguments which continue into the next chapter; and at the end of the latter, Gulliver delivers a few sentences on the political history of Brobdingnag. Those closing sentences of Gulliver's sound very much like a work which Swift published in 1701, *A Discourse of the Contests and Dissensions*; and this relationship has a special meaning.

The link between Brobdingnagian political history and Swift's *Discourse* was noted by Professor Case; but another scholar, Professor Robert Joseph Allen, had already shown what I consider to be the significance of this link. In a study of the *Discourse*, Professor Allen demonstrated that Swift's

---

[1] Stanza vii.   [2] *Gulliver*, pp. 180-1, 174; *Ode*, stanzas v and vi.
[3] *Gulliver*, p. 181; *Ode*, stanzas i and iv; Sir Henry Craik, *Life of Jonathan Swift* (2nd ed., London, 1894), I, 95.

book was founded upon certain works by Sir William Temple; and it is in fact possible to trace themes back from *Brobdingnag* to Temple's essays either directly or through the intermediate stage of the *Discourse*.[1] I shall give only two of the simplest illustrations.

There is a particularly neat, triangular relationship among the following specimens: Gulliver gives the giant king a most flattering account of the House of Commons. The king asks,

> How it came to pass, that people were so violently bent upon getting into this assembly ... often to the ruin of their families, without any salary or pension: because this appeared such an exalted strain of virtue and publick spirit, that his majesty seemed to doubt it might possibly not be always sincere: And he desired to know whether such zealous gentlemen could have any views of refunding themselves for the charges and trouble they were at, by sacrificing the publick good to the designs of ... a corrupted ministry.

Temple, writing on popular assemblies, had said,

> The needy, the ambitious ... the covetous, are ever restless to get into public employments. .... I have found no talent of so much advantage among men, towards their growing great or rich, as a violent and restless passion and pursuit for one or the other. .... Yet all these cover their ends with most worthy pretences, and those noble sayings, That men are not born for themselves, and must sacrifice their lives for the public, as well as their time and health.

[1] See Case's edition of *Gulliver* (New York, 1938), p. 142n; and Allen's 'Swift's Earliest Political Tract and Sir William Temple's Essays', *Harvard Studies and Notes in Philology and Literature*, XIX (1937), 3–12. Mr Myrddin Jones, in his thesis (see above, p. 62, note 1), adds further evidence. The stages of the relationship may be traced in, first, Temple's essays 'On the Original and Nature of Government' and 'Of Popular Discontents'; secondly, Chapters I and V of Swift's *Discourse*; and third, Chapters VI and VII of *Brobdingnag*.

The passage here quoted from Temple is part of a longer
section picked out by Professor Allen as having influenced
Swift's *Discourse*.[1]

The King of Brobdingnag also asked Gulliver about the
English army. The innuendo of his question is that a paid
army in peace time is needed only to maintain the power
of a tyrant:

> Above all, he was amazed to hear me talk of a mercenary
> standing army in the midst of peace, and among a free people.
> He said, if we were governed by our own consent in the per-
> sons of our representatives, he could not imagine of whom we
> were afraid, or against whom we were to fight, and would
> hear my opinion, whether a private man's house might not
> better be defended by himself, his children, and family, than
> by half a dozen rascals picked up at a venture in the streets, for
> small wages.

Temple, in his essay on government, says that a king and
his people are like a father and his family; so a just and careful
parent is willingly followed and obeyed by all his children.
But a tyrant thinks he cannot be safe among his children,
except by putting arms into the hands of hired servants:

> For against a foreign enemy, and for defence of evident
> interest, all that can bear arms in a nation are soldiers . . . and
> these kind of forces [i.e., mercenaries] come to be used by good
> princes, only upon necessity of providing for their defence
> against great and armed neighbours or enemies; but by ill
> ones as a support of decayed authority, or as they lose the force
> of that which is natural and paternal. . . .
>
> Yet this seems a much weaker principle of government . . .
> [for] common pay is a faint principle of courage and action,
> in comparison of religion, liberty, honour, revenge, or
> necessity . . . so as if the people come to unite by any strong

[1] *Gulliver*, p. 173; Temple, *Works* (London, 1770), III, 42-43; Allen, pp. 9-10.

passion, or general interest . . . they are masters of [mercenary] armies.[1]

Most of the giant king's discussion of politics has a similar parallel in Temple's essays on government.

Now there should really be nothing to surprise one in Swift's reviving, for *Gulliver's Travels*, the ideas of his earlier work. The situation of his three great friends – Bolingbroke, Oxford, and Ormonde – in 1715 seemed to repeat the circumstances which had provoked the *Discourse*. In 1701 four former ministers were most unfairly impeached by the House of Commons, but they were dismissed and acquitted by the Lords. Swift thought the impeachments outrageous, and wrote his *Discourse* to prove them so. In 1715, his own ministerial friends were impeached. Though he might write a book then, however, nobody would dare to print it, and even *his* head was not out of danger. When, in 1721-2, he transmuted these memories within a satiric fantasy, the arguments hardly changed, and their origin remained, ultimately, Sir William Temple.

In *Brobdingnag*, however, as in *Lilliput*, the seeds of a writer's imagination should not be treated as the product. While Swift's patron may have been a partial forebear of the giant king, this Voyage carries its own import, quite separate from any facts of Temple's life. Though less vicious than the pigmies, the Brobdingnagians possess a fair complement of human weaknesses. The now minute traveller finds that error abounds even among the 'least corrupted' of mankind,[2] and that no fleshly charms can stand up to a sufficiently microscopic inspection. Again, reversing Gulliver's field of

---

[1] *Gulliver*, pp. 174-5; Temple, *Works*, I, 45. Professor H. W. Donner has kindly pointed out to me that this motif is one more sign of *Gulliver's* connection (often slighted) with More's *Utopia* (Book II, Chapter 8).   [2] *Gulliver*, p. 414.

vision, the sagacious reader may also infer the continuation of Pascal's logic: 'Qui n'admirera que notre corps, qui tantôt n'était pas perceptible dans l'univers . . . soit à présent un colosse, un monde, ou plutôt un tout, à l'égard du néant où l'on ne peut arriver?'[1]

IV

For Houyhnhnmland (the third part of *Gulliver* in order of composition) my reasoning depends on two related assumptions. The first is that although the houyhnhnms embody traits which Swift admired, they do not represent his moral ideal for mankind. The other is that the houyhnhnms combine deistic and stoic views of human nature – views against which, as a devout Anglican, he fought. By 'deistic' I mean the vague tradition in which men like Swift tended to lump free thinkers, deists, Socinians, and some Latitudinarians. The term 'deist' was seldom used with any precision in the eighteenth century. Bolingbroke would not have admitted to the title, although his works were normally received as subversive of Christianity. Avowed deists were extremely rare, but Swift threw the label about with great freedom. By 'stoic' I mean the doctrine of disinterested virtue, with its emphasis on man's self-sufficiency, its advocacy of a life without passion, its impossible and un-Christian goal of indifference to grief, death, and other misfortunes. But I shall not attempt to distinguish between these traditions because they are intimately blended in the reasoning of both their adherents and their opponents.[2]

Even a hasty reader might notice signs which support my

[1] Pascal, p. 37.
[2] See Louis Landa's 'Introduction to the Sermons', in Davis, IX, 108-14.

assumptions. A rather light hint is the houyhnhnms' ignorance of bodily shame: Gulliver says he asked his houyhnhnm master's forgiveness

> if I did not expose those parts, that nature taught us to conceal. He said ∴ . . he could not understand why nature should teach us to conceal what nature had given.[1]

Here, Gulliver's error resides in his logic rather than his modesty. It was not nature that taught us to conceal our genitalia; it was a supernatural moral law.

A more serious clue is a saying of Gulliver's master, that '*Reason* alone is sufficient to govern a *rational* creature.'[2] This maxim runs contrary to the spirit of Christianity: except by removing men from the category of 'rational creatures', no sincere Anglican could agree with the wise houyhnhnm. Swift devotes two of his extant sermons to annihilating such doctrines, and these sermons are the best of all commentaries on Houyhnhnmland. He excludes the possibility of virtue without Christianity except through rare 'personal merit', as in Socrates and Cato, who happened to be blessed with a disposition (not reason) naturally good. 'There is no solid, firm foundation of virtue, but in a conscience directed by the principles of religion.'[3]

Deistic philosophers run in another direction. William Wollaston, one of Swift's detestations, writes,

> To act according to right reason, and to act according to truth are in effect the same thing. . . . To be governed by reason is the general law imposed by the author of nature upon them, whose uppermost faculty is reason.[4]

[1] *Gulliver*, p. 333.   [2] *Gulliver*, p. 367.
[3] 'On the Testimony of Conscience' and 'Upon the Excellency of Christianity'. See Davis, IX, 249, 154.
[4] *The Religion of Nature Delineated* (London, 1722), p. 36.

Similarly, the inexhaustible benevolence of the houyhnhnms sounds, even *prima facie*, like a parody of such antecedents of deism as the Earl of Shaftesbury, who says,

> To deserve the name of good or virtuous, a creature must have all his inclinations and affections, his dispositions of mind and temper, suitable, and agreeing with the good of his kind . . . this affection of a creature toward the good of the species or common nature is . . . proper and natural to him.[1]

Shaftesbury is at pains to show that the Christian doctrine of rewards and punishments can be inconsistent with virtue. It is also suggestive that William Godwin, one of the fullest flowers of the deistic tradition, should have been infatuated with the houyhnhnms, calling them a description of 'men in their highest improvement', and finding in Swift's exposition of their government 'a more profound insight into the true principles of political justice, than [in] any preceding or contemporary author'.[2]

Swift, for more than fifty years, was a priest in the Church of England. There is no doubt that he took his responsibilities as a pastor more seriously than most of his clerical colleagues took theirs. He reformed the worship in his cathedral to make it more regular and fuller than it had been for many years. He prayed in secret, went to church early so as not to be seen, wrote for his dearest friend some prayers which are models of intense but traditional religious expression. He gave a third of his income to charity and saved half the remainder to leave a fortune to charity. His sermons, the

---

[1] *Characteristicks*, ed. J. M. Robertson (London, 1900), I, 280. Of course, Shaftesbury, in spite of his influence, was a sound Christian.

[2] *The Inquirer* (London, 1797), p. 134; *Political Justice*, ed. F. E. L. Priestley (Toronto, 1946), II, 209n. For detailed evidence, see James Preu, 'Swift's Influence on Godwin's Doctrine of Anarchism', *Journal of the History of Ideas*, XV (1954), 371-83.

remarks of his intimates, his own private papers, all confirm Swift's devotion to his faith and his calling. Nevertheless, he had suffered so many accusations of impiety – from misinterpreters of *A Tale of a Tub* and other works – that he would not bring religion openly into a satire like *Gulliver.*

In providing the houyhnhnms with good qualities, he was therefore duplicating the method of More's *Utopia*; and, to only this extent, R. W. Chambers is correct in writing,

> Just as More scored a point against the wickedness of Christian Europe, by making his philosophers heathen, so Jonathan Swift scored a point against the wickedness of mankind by representing *his* philosophers, the Houyhnhnms, as having the bodies of horses.[1]

So, in his sermon 'On the Excellency of Christianity', Swift argues that although there were 'great examples of wisdom and virtue among the heathen wise men', nevertheless, 'Christian philosophy is in all things preferable to heathen wisdom'.[2] As admirable creatures, the houyhnhnms represent beings (neither horses nor men) capable of pursuing the natural virtues summed up in reason and given us by nature at one remove from God; in their way – which is not the human way – they are perfect, and do not want religion. As absurd creatures, they represent the deistic presumption that mankind has no need of the specifically Christian virtues. Gulliver is misled as, in *Joseph Andrews*, 'Mr Wilson' is ruined by a club of 'philosophers' who 'governed themselves only by the infallible guide of human reason', but who reveal their immorality when one of them withdraws, 'taking with him the wife of one of his most intimate friends', and another refuses to pay back a loan which 'Mr Wilson'

---

[1] *Sir Thomas More* (London, 1935), p. 128.   [2] Davis, IX, 243.

had made to him. While under the spell, the victim says,

> I began now to esteem myself a being of a higher order than
> I had ever before conceived; and was more charmed with this
> rule of right, as I really found in my own nature nothing repug-
> nant to it. I held in utter contempt all persons who wanted any
> other inducement to virtue besides her intrinsic beauty and
> excellence.[1]

Gulliver is not defrauded by the houyhnhnms, for they are
not human (or equine); but the rule of nothing-but-reason
leads him to repudiate all human obligations and to detest
his wife. Swift wished men to be as rational as possible; he
believed that religion helps them to become so, and that
reason leads them toward revelation. But the deistic effort
to build a rational system of morals outside revelation, he
regarded as evil and absurd.

V

In the fourth voyage, Swift was probably aiming at a
particular exponent of deistic thought, a correspondent with
whom he had arguments about such doctrines while he was
writing *Gulliver's Travels*. To identify the person, I shall
limit myself at first to the most striking attributes of the
houyhnhnms: their emotionless serenity, their benevolence,
and their reliance on reason.

Of the houyhnhnms' indifference to such feelings as fear
of death or filial love, one needs no reminding; this superi-
ority to human passions appears throughout the fourth
voyage. In Chapter VIII Gulliver surveys some of their other
felicities. '*Friendship* and *benevolence*', he says,

---

[1] Fielding's *Works*, ed. W. E. Henley (London, 1903), I, 240-1 (Book III,
Chapter 3).

are the two principal virtues among the houyhnhnms; and these not confined to particular objects, but universal to the whole race. For, a stranger from the remotest part, is equally treated with the nearest neighbour, and where-ever he goes, looks upon himself as at home. . . . They will have it that *nature* teaches them to love the whole species, and it is *reason* only that maketh a distinction of persons, where there is a superior degree of virtue.[1]

In 1719 Swift re-opened a correspondence with Bolingbroke which had been suspended for more than two years. In his answer Bolingbroke has a long passage on friendship, to which Swift replied in detail. After another exchange, the correspondence once more lapsed. When Swift wrote again, Bolingbroke sent him a very long letter which included further and extended reflections on friendship, such as,

Believe me, there is more pleasure, and more merit too, in cultivating friendship, than in taking care of the state . . . none but men of sense and virtue are capable of [it].[2]

It was Bolingbroke who wrote a whole treatise to prove that compassion, or kindness to strangers, depends on reason and nothing else; and in it he made such remarks as, 'An habit of making good use of our reason, and such an education as trains up the mind in true morality, will never fail to inspire us with sentiments of benevolence for all mankind'. In another essay he has declarations like, 'Sociability is the great instinct, and benevolence the great law, of human nature.'[3]

In Bolingbroke's next letter, he placed Swift on the opposite side of a quarrel about the Christian religion and

---

[1] *Gulliver*, pp. 379-80.   [2] See Ball, III, 24-30, 89.
[3] *Reflections concerning Innate Moral Principles* (London, 1752), p. 55; *Philosophical Works* (London, 1754), IV, 256.

ancient morality. He harps on the theme that 'a man of sense and virtue may be unfortunate, but can never be unhappy'. Almost two years later (August 1723), Swift received a double letter from Pope and Bolingbroke, both dilating on friendship; Pope's has so many maxims relating to this subject that it is more an essay than a letter. The two men emphasize their contentment, their indifference to ordinary vicissitudes, their philosophical serenity. They preach a cool moderation remote from the ordeals of Swift's preceding year. 'Reflection and habit', wrote Bolingbroke,

> have rendered the world so indifferent to me, that I am neither afflicted nor rejoiced, angry nor pleased, at what happens in it. . . . Perfect tranquility is the general tenor of my life.[1]

While Swift may have envied such complacency, he could not imitate it. He sent a sarcastic riposte ridiculing their pretensions to detached and philosophic calm. 'Your notions of friendship are new to me,' Swift says; 'I believe every man is born with his *quantum*, and he cannot give to one without robbing another.' As for their nonchalance, he told Pope, 'I who am sunk under the prejudices of another education . . . can never arrive at the serenity of mind you possess.' It was their sort of vapidity that Swift meant to deride, two years later, when he jeered at how Bolingbroke in 1723 had been 'full of philosophy, and talked *de contemptu mundi*'.[2]

The next development of the correspondence seems related to Gulliver's most often-quoted comment on the houyhnhnms, his praise of their devotion to reason (i.e., to reason alone):

---

[1] Ball, III, III, 172.   [2] Ball, III, 175, 291.

As these noble houyhnhnms are endowed by nature with a general disposition to all virtues, and have no conceptions . . . of what is evil in a rational creature, so their grand maxim is, to cultivate *reason*, and to be wholly governed by it. Neither is *reason* among them a point problematical as with us, where men can argue with plausibility on both sides of the question; but strikes you with immediate conviction; as it must needs do where it is not mingled, obscured, or discoloured by passion and interest.[1]

In the autumn of 1724, the undercurrent of Swift's quarrel with his friend becomes traceable; and it flows about this very problem of what reason unaided can do. Bolingbroke sent a long defence of deistic thought and an attack on Christianity (by implication), to rebut a letter that is now lost, from Swift. The dean had directly accused him of being an *esprit fort*, or free thinker.[2] In a tremendous harangue, Bolingbroke first takes the word to mean atheist, and repudiates that title; then he says, among similar remarks,

If indeed by *esprit fort*, or free-thinker, you only mean a man who makes a free use of his reason, who searches after truth without passion or prejudice, and adheres inviolably to it, you mean a wise and honest man, and such a one as I labour to be. The faculty of distinguishing between right and wrong, true and false, which we call reason or common sense, which is given to every man by our bountiful creator, and which most men lose by neglect, is the light of the mind, and ought to guide all the operations of it. To abandon this rule, and to guide our thoughts by any other [Bolingbroke means Christian revelation], is full as absurd as it would be, if you should put out your eyes, and borrow even the best staff . . . when you set out upon one of your dirty journeys. . . . The peace and happiness of mankind is the great aim of these free-thinkers.[3]

[1] *Gulliver*, pp. 378-9.   [2] *Letters to Ford*, pp. 100-1.
[3] Ball, III, 208-9. That Bolingbroke means Christian revelation is clear from his parallel with Locke's *Essay concerning Human Understanding*, IV, xix, 4, 8.

In Bolingbroke's philosophical works there are many other similarities to the teachings of the houyhnhnms. In fact, Gulliver's list of the subjects which generally come up in their conversations could serve almost as well for those works: friendship and benevolence, order and 'oeconomy', the visible operations of nature, ancient traditions, the bounds and limits of virtue, the unerring rules of reason, etc.[1] Of course, however, Swift omits the purpose of Bolingbroke philosophizing, which (according to his eighteenth-century critics) was the destruction of Christianity. Swift believed that a good Christian is a rational person, that reason leads one to Christian faith, that these two gifts are in harmony, and that man must strive to enlarge them both.

One final touch is that Bolingbroke's editor calls his philosophical writings for the most part 'nothing more than repetitions of conversations often interrupted, [and] often renewed'.[2] For I have assumed that the letters from Bolingbroke had the effect of reminding Swift of topics more freely canvassed when the two men had talked together.[3]

Although my observations pause here, there is a humorous postscript to the houyhnhnms. Viscount Bolingbroke was no horse, and it would have been convenient to discover one which was not only a deistic thinker but also a master of human beings. By a helpful chance, it happens that Swift once described such an animal, in a letter. The episode may be no more than an odd coincidence, but it seems worth reporting. For on this occasion Swift's horse behaved more

---

[1] *Gulliver*, p. 393.   [2] *Philosophical Works*, III, 334.
[3] D. G. James saw the connection between the houyhnhnms and Bolingbroke, but he quite misunderstood it; see his *Life of Reason* (London, 1949), pp. 256-61. I am indebted to Miss Kathleen Williams for this reference. Miss Williams, whose book on Swift will soon be ready, has come to conclusions like my own as to the meaning of the fourth voyage.

rationally than his servant, and the master treated the man like an animal.

At Christmas time, 1714, the dean rode out of Dublin, planning to collect his groom and his valet on the way. When he met them, they were incapably drunk; and he found that the groom could not travel. Swift nevertheless rode on, but noticed that Tom, the valet, who usually rode behind him, failed to keep up. He waited, and Tom galloped to him. Swift scolded him, and Tom answered foolishly. 'He was as drunk as a dog,' Swift wrote,

> tottered on his horse, could not keep the way, sometimes into the sea, then back to me; swore he was not drunk. I bid him keep on, lashed him as well as I could; then he vowed he was drunk, fell a crying, came back every moment to me. I bid him keep on.

At last, from the galloping and turning backwards and forwards, Tom's horse 'grew mad' and threw the valet down. Then Swift came up and called a boy and man to get the horse from him; but

> he resisted us all three, was stark mad with drink. At last we got the bridle from him, the boy mounted and away we rode, Tom following after us. What became of him I know not.[1]

The episode has a peculiar interest, not only because the horse was English and the servants Irish, but because the name of the horse which 'grew mad' and threw Tom down was Bolingbroke. The editor of Swift's correspondence says that the horse Bolingbroke was a gift, and that Swift named him; but we do not know who the donor was. In June 1713, Vanessa asked Swift, 'How does Bolingbroke perform?' Swift, en route to Ireland, said the horse fell under him;

[1] Ball, II, 263.

and in the end it was shipped over to its new country. Swift mentions Bolingbroke several times again, but after three years he exchanged him for another horse. We never heard of him again, unless perhaps in *Gulliver's Travels*.[1]

But the refutation of Bolingbroke is merely a component of this Voyage, throwing a less interesting light upon its meaning than on the history of its composition. Swift's implications go further, in Part IV, than anywhere else in *Gulliver*. If the houyhnhnms are a false ideal for humanity, the yahoos are a false debasement of our nature. The representation of men as apes suggests Calvinist doctrines. In depicting our case as hopeless, and denying our power in any way to move toward salvation except through the arbitrary action of unmerited, unpredictable grace, the Puritans sink us to the category of mindless beasts. As the truly Christian alternative to both deistic and Dissenting errors, Swift provides Captain Pedro de Mendez, 'the finest of all the European characters' in *Gulliver*.[2] It is in this image of humility, compassion, and charity (disdained by the infatuated Gulliver) that he would like us to rest. 'Connaissons donc notre portée; nous sommes quelque chose, et ne sommes pas tout.'[3]

VI

Swift began to write the third voyage (last in order of composition) around January 1724, and he returned to Dublin, that month, from a visit which he had made to Quilca, the country home of his young and very dear friend,

---

[1] Ball, II, 44 & n, 45 & n, 242, 280-1, 305-6.
[2] Case, *Four Essays*, p. 121.   [3] Pascal, p. 39.

the Reverend Thomas Sheridan. Swift may have visited Quilca again the following April. Meanwhile, the *Drapier's Letters* interrupted the writing of *Gulliver*; and Swift only finished the third voyage some time in 1725. At Quilca again the whole book was perfected and rewritten when Swift stayed there from April to the end of September, 1725.

Sheridan provided Swift with more than a holiday. He gave him a model for the king and people of the flying island. Swift had met him in 1718, and their twenty-year friendship was perhaps never stronger than during the period when *Gulliver* was being written and they were meeting constantly in Dublin. Yet Swift found fault with his friend almost from the start. In letters, poems, and other papers, Swift continually bewailed Sheridan's absent-mindedness, his inability to listen carefully during conversations, his irresponsibility and forgetfulness, his neglect of the essential business of life in favour of peripheral occupations.

'Too much advertency is not your talent,' Swift told Sheridan. And, 'I believe you value your temporal interest as much as anybody, but you have not the arts of pursuing it.' And again, 'The two devils of inadvertency and forgetfulness have got fast hold on you.' Describing him at the same time to another acquaintance, Swift wrote, 'He hath not overmuch advertency. His books, his mathematics, the pressures of his fortune, his laborious calling, and some natural disposition or indisposition, give him an *egarement d'esprit*, as you cannot but observe.'[1]

In brief, Sheridan possessed to an extreme degree the characteristic on which Gulliver builds his portrait of the Laputans – that their minds are

[1] Ball, III, 267, 268, 275, 271.

so taken up with intense speculations, that they neither can speak, nor attend to the discourses of others, without being rouzed.[1]

Instead of caring for their common affairs, the Laputans and their king occupy themselves with three obsessions: music, mathematics, and abstract speculation. Swift described Sheridan as 'a man of intent and abstracted thinking, enslaved by mathematics'.[2] Sheridan's own son writes,

> As he was an adept in music both in the scientific and practical part, he had frequent private concerts at his house at no small cost.[3]

The King of Laputa was 'distinguished above all his predecessors for his hospitality to strangers'.[4] Sheridan's son says his father was recklessly hospitable and generous:

> [He] set no bounds to his prodigality. . . . [He had a] large income . . . but not equal to the profuseness of his spirit. He was . . . the greatest dupe in the world and a constant prey to all the indigent of his acquaintance, as well as those who were recommended to him by others.[5]

Swift used to berate Sheridan for wasting money on the entertainment of false friends and random acquaintances.[6]

Sheridan also shared the Laputans' fecklessness in the management of his property. 'It is [his] great happiness,' Swift once observed of him,

> that, when he acts in the common concerns of life against common sense and reason, he values himself thereupon, as if it were the mark of great genius, above little regards or arts, and that his thoughts are too exalted to descend into the knowledge of vulgar management; and you cannot make him a greater compliment than by telling instances to the company,

[1] *Gulliver*, pp. 217-18.   [2] Ball, III, 268.
[3] Thomas Sheridan, *Life of Jonathan Swift* (London, 1784), pp. 384-5.
[4] *Gulliver*, p. 219.   [5] Sheridan, p. 384.   [6] Ball, III, 246, 268.

before his face, how careless he was in any affair that related to his interest and fortune.[1]

Gulliver blames the same defects in the Laputans:

> Although they are dextrous enough upon a piece of paper . . . yet in the common actions and behaviour of life, I have not seen a more clumsy, awkward, and unhandy people, nor so slow and perplexed in their conceptions upon all other subjects, except those of mathematicks and musick.[2]

In the same portrait in which he analysed Sheridan's pride at being incompetent, Swift also described him as proud, captious, quarrelsome, and argumentative. After remarking that the Laputans are hopeless fumblers in practical affairs, Gulliver says, 'They are very bad reasoners, and vehemently given to opposition, unless when they happen to be of the right opinion.'[3]

Finally, there is the famous description by Gulliver of the desolation on the mainland subject to the King of Laputa: 'I never knew a soil so unhappily cultivated, houses so ill contrived and so ruinous,' etc.[4] While Swift was writing *Gulliver's Travels*, he also composed verses ridiculing the miserable conditions of agriculture and buildings at Quilca:

> *A rotten cabbin, dropping rain . . .*
> *Stools, tables, chairs, and bed-steds broke:*
> *Here elements have lost their uses,*
> *Air ripens not, nor earth produces. . . .*

Or, in another poem of the same time on the same subject:

> *A church without pews.*
> *Our horses astray,*
> *No straw, oats, or hay;*
> *December in May.*[5]

---

[1] *Prose Works*, ed. T. Scott, XI, 156.   [2] *Gulliver*, pp. 223-4.
[3] *Prose Works*, ed. T. Scott, XI, 156-8; *Gulliver*, p. 224.
[4] *Gulliver*, p. 241.   [5] *Poems*, III, 1035, 1036.

There is as well a prose diatribe dated April 1724, *The Blunders, Deficiencies, Distresses, and Misfortunes of Quilca*. Here Swift denounces the crazy state of the house and all its furniture, the lack of food, heat, and comfort, the savage behaviour of the servants, the barbaric manners of the natives: 'The new house all going to ruin before it is finished. . . . The kitchen perpetually crowded with savages. . . . Not a bit of mutton to be had in the country. . . . An egregious want of all the most common necessary utensils. . . . [The servants] growing fast into the manners and thieveries of the natives.' In Balnibarbi, 'the whole country lies miserably wast, the houses in ruins, and the people without food or cloths.'[1]

There are many additional hints and clues to demonstrate the conclusion. Swift was not thinking *only* of Sheridan when he described the Laputans, but he was thinking more deeply of him than of anyone else.

Nevertheless, the third voyage is not a study of Quilca or of Thomas Sheridan. For Swift, Sheridan constituted a single example of the faults which were destroying Ireland. By not assuming the moral burden of enfranchised citizens, the Irish landlords, politicians, and intellectual leaders were letting their country collapse. To the dean, the pure research of astronomers or mathematicians seemed like frivolous evasions of real duties. In Irish poverty and slavery, he foresaw the fate of England as well. Like the vision of the *Dunciad IV*, Laputa signifies a condemnation of political, scientific, and moral irresponsibility. For England the symptoms include the Bubble, the Royal Society, the Walpole-Townshend feud, and the personal vices of George I; for

[1] *Prose Works*, ed. T. Scott, XI, 75-77; *Gulliver*, p. 244.

Ireland, the decay of agriculture, industry, and trade. In such a scene, to busy oneself with fantastic inquiries and useless experiments appeared criminal: 'Si l'homme s'étudiait le premier, il verrait combien il est incapable de passer outre.'[1]

VII

I am far from supposing that persons in *Gulliver's Travels* are portraits of men whom Swift knew. The King of Brobdingnag is not Sir William Temple; nor is Thomas Sheridan the King of Laputa. In all the characters there are elements inconsistent with the originals that I have put forward. I suggest merely that the framework of the houyhnhnms' character, for instance, goes back to Bolingbroke; that the giant king is derived from Swift's recollections of Temple, though with many additions and alterations; and so forth.

The most important question is how these observations alter one's reading of *Gulliver's Travels*. But to this the answers are so ramified that I shall no more than list a few implications. My analysis of the second voyage may go far to account for its *relative* placidity and its success, in comparison with the contemptuous tone of the first, the disjointedness of the third, and the harshness of the fourth; Swift had returned to the mood of his satisfying and fruitful years with Temple at Moor Park. The third voyage is one which has often been related to Scriblerian sketches; and an explanation for its inadequacy has been that here Swift was stitching up ill-connected fragments. My association of the Laputan king with Thomas Sheridan weakens that theory. Other scholars have shown that the political references and

[1] Pascal, p. 41.

much of the satire on experimental science belong to the later part of the reign of George I; so does the connection with Sheridan.[1] My commentary on the fourth voyage helps to destroy the misconceptions of innumerable scholars and critics who identify the author, through Gulliver, with the values of the houyhnhnms. Swift was himself saying, in the fourth voyage, that anyone who believes in the adequacy of reason without Christianity must see himself as a houyhnhnm and the rest of mankind as yahoos. By innuendo, he argues that the deists and neo-stoics cannot, with any consistency, believe their own doctrines.[2]

Finally, I suggest that the common approaches to Swift's satire, with an emphasis on manipulation of ideas, or else in terms of technique of fiction, usually mislead one. Swift's imagination worked in terms of people. He did not invent a set of values to defend, or objects to attack; he started from human embodiments of those values or vices, and he addressed himself to people whom he wished to encourage, refute, or annihilate.

To consider *Gulliver's Travels* as a novel, to present it in language evolved for the criticism of prose fiction, and to study Swift's 'personae' as people, is to misunderstand this book. *Gulliver* is admittedly an ancestor of stories like *Erewhon* and *Brave New World*. Swift, however, was writing a prose satire according to another form, curiously static and didactic, but not narrative as an epic or novel is. Its structure and its repetitive pattern help to explain both why

---

[1] Case, *Four Essays*, passim; Marjorie Nicolson and N. M. Mohler, 'The Scientific Background of Swift's Voyage to Laputa', *Annals of Science*, II (1937), 299-334.

[2] I am indebted to Dr Theodore Redpath for a discussion clarifying this statement.

it succeeds as a children's book and why it cannot be made into a satisfactory film or drama. Very little of the life in *Gulliver* belongs to its large 'story' or 'plot' line, or to the evolution of character. The life comes from the detached characterizations of individuals who otherwise exist as flat masks or as spokesmen and mouthpieces; from separate episodes loosely strung together; and, most of all, from the operations of Swift's irony.

Gulliver's characterizations are like the portraits in Swift's *History of the Four Last Years*, where he analyses statesmen in order to account for actions which the reader has already learned about outside the book: the motives, one might say, are revealed after the action is over and not through it – to explain and not to initiate it. So in *Gulliver* most episodes move independently of the characterizations and of one another. What if the King of Brobdingnag did dislike armies and had no use for them? He nevertheless possessed a militia of 200,000 men; and all of Gulliver's apologizing does not convince me that Swift put that army in for any other reason than to enhance the giant king's awsomeness at the expense of his coherence. One finds consistency in neither the chronology, the geography, nor the characters of this fable; its true coherence rests on the moral pattern, the chain of values which the author advocates. If Swift had embodied these in consistent symbolic figures, the result would have been hollow personifications; but he did not. Instead, he designed his portraits around vital impressions of people whom he knew, and they have become immortal.

Chapter Six

MADNESS

We all have learned that Swift went mad. Even those who cannot identify Stella know this. But not many lunatics have had Swift's good luck. His case was reported at once; and his symptoms have been sketched by no less than four famous writers, of whom three are generally labelled great and one brilliant: Johnson, Scott, Thackeray, and Huxley. If he had written nothing but a will, such attention must have guaranteed a place for him in the manuals of English literature.

One of the earliest accounts comes from a letter written three years before Swift's death, by Charles Yorke, son of the first Lord Hardwicke; he says,

> Dean Swift has had a statute of lunacy taken out against him. His madness appears chiefly in most incessant strains of obscenity and swearing; habits . . . of which his writings have some tincture.[1]

Johnson, who probably knew of this report, traced the decay back to 1736, nine years before the end: Swift's ideas, he says, 'wore gradually away, and left his mind vacant', until his anger was at last 'heightened into madness'. This condition, according to Johnson, was 'compounded of rage and

---

[1] John, Lord Campbell, *Lives of the Lord Chancellors* (London, 1847), II, 20-21.

fatuity', and Swift finally reached a 'lethargick stupidity, motionless, heedless, and speechless'.[1]

Scott, with more information, could state authoritatively that Swift's understanding failed soon after 1740, and his state became that of 'violent and furious lunacy'. From this 'outrageous frenzy, aggravated by bodily suffering', says Scott, Swift sank into 'the situation of a helpless changeling'.[2]

Thackeray is interested to show foreshadowings of the unsavory denouement; and he points out the insane tendencies of Swift's whole career – 'the storms and tempests of his furious mind . . . the maddened hurricane of his life'. Swift, Thackeray says, went 'through life, tearing, like a man possessed with a devil'. Swift knows 'that the night will come and the inevitable hag with it. What a night, my God, it was! what a lonely rage and long agony.'[3]

Huxley, aided by the psychological insights of our century, has an essay quite as dazzling as Thackeray's but more precise in its interpretations:

> Swift must have 'hated the word bowels' to the verge of insanity. . . . Swift hated bowels with such a passionate abhorrence that he felt a perverse compulsion to bathe continually in the squelchy imagination of them.
>
> Swift's greatness lies in the intensity, the almost insane violence of that 'hatred of bowels' which is the essence of his misanthropy and which underlies the whole of his work.[4]

Swift's most recent biographer, Middleton Murry, tells essentially the same story. By the end of 1738, 'Swift was not fully responsible for his own actions'. He was, says

[1] *Lives of the Poets* (Everyman edition, London, 1925), II, 265-6.
[2] *Memoirs of Jonathan Swift* (2nd ed., Edinburgh, 1824), pp. 451-4.
[3] *The English Humourists* (London, 1853), pp. 31-32.
[4] 'Swift', in *Do What You Will* (London, 1929), pp. 94, 99.

Murry, 'under the terrible and now imminent menace of imbecility'.[1]

We have read other analyses, more sober perhaps, and more cautious, but much duller. Of the consensus, there can be no doubt. Swift's life was marked by insane tendencies; and as he grew older, he grew wilder, ending in madness.

What can one add to this outline? I believe that I can supply facts of chronology and perhaps etiology that will significantly modify it. For example, when did Swift go mad? This in its turn is a simple question only if we can agree that certain things are not madness. Swift had a bad memory all his life. It grew worse as he aged. It was so poor when he was in his early forties that he misdated works which he had written ten years and less before he published them in 1711. Since many scholars and scientists are shockingly forgetful, his trait can hardly be a mark of the imbecile.

Swift also had a neurological complaint which he failed to diagnose correctly. In fact, it was not understood until many years after his death. This is labyrinthine vertigo, or Ménière's Syndrome. The disease attacks the inner ear, causing either deafness or vertigo or both. Its origin is unknown; it can start at various ages, with no warning, and comes in recurrent spells which may grow more unpleasant and more extended as the victim ages. Today one finds sufferers reporting it as coming on suddenly. They may have violent fits of vomiting; often they feel too dizzy to stand up; and they sometimes lose their hearing. As a palliative, they take daily the pills prescribed against seasickness; and then they usually have no trouble. There isn't any cure. Cutting the aural nerve ends the symptoms but of course

[1] *Jonathan Swift* (London, 1954), pp. 479-80.

makes the patient permanently deaf. There is no connection between Ménière's disease and insanity.

Swift often complained of his poor memory, his deafness, and his nauseous seizures. These complaints, in his later years, are sometimes very little restrained. He wrote about them to several friends who saved his letters, so that we have a little collection of outbursts delivered while he was overcome by his sickness: for example –

> I have been very miserable all night, and to-day extremely deaf and full of pain. I am so stupid and confounded, that I cannot express the mortification I am under both in body and mind. All I can say is, that I am not in torture, but I daily and hourly expect it.[1]

Swift's misery was aggravated by his unwillingness to let visitors or friends witness the agony. His eyes weakened, and he refused to wear glasses; so he found reading very difficult, using books printed only in the largest type. It is not pleasant to imagine how he may have felt at the age of seventy-three, five years before his death, lying deaf in bed, with surges of nausea and retching, unable for days to receive a friend or read a book. Yet all this is not yet insanity.

One more punishment remains. Shortly before Swift's seventy-fifth birthday, one of his eyes became badly swollen; he had a general outbreak of boils; he was delirious and in torment for a week; although he could eat, he hardly slept for a month. There is no mystery about this siege. It has been diagnosed by one of Britain's most distinguished neurologists, Sir Walter Russell Brain, as orbital cellulitis – a

[1] Ball, VI, 165.

feverish and most painful inflammation of the tissue lining the eye socket.[1] The infection is purely physiological and has nothing to do with insanity.

Now the way seems clear. Bad memory, poor eyesight, deafness, Ménière's Syndrome, orbital cellulitis – beyond all these, our opening question remains: When did Swift go mad? There are several means of telling. As Dean of St Patrick's Cathedral, he had many duties to perform, and some of these were recorded. So long as Swift could, he presided over meetings of the cathedral chapter; but in July 1739, he chose a subdean, because he himself was so often incapacitated. Several later meetings were transferred from the chapter house to the deanery in order that Swift might be on hand. The last time this happened, he was in the middle of his seventy-fifth year.[2] About two months before, he had written an order directing the vicars choral not to participate in a musical society without the permission of the subdean and chapter of St Patrick's. A paragraph of this exhortation is worth reading as a taste of the last of Swift's public utterances:

> And whereas it hath been reported, that I gave a licence to certain vicars to assist at a club of fiddlers in Fishamble Street, I do hereby declare that I remember no such licence to have been ever signed or sealed by me; and that if ever such pretended licence should be produced, I do hereby annul and vacate the said licence; intreating my said Sub-Dean and Chapter to punish such vicars as shall ever appear there, as songsters, fiddlers, pipers, trumpeters, drummers, drum-majors, or in any sonal quality, according to the flagitious

[1] W. R. Brain, 'The Illness of Dean Swift', *Irish Journal of Medical Science*, August-September 1952, pp. 337-46.
[2] Louis Landa, *Swift and the Church of Ireland* (Oxford, 1954), p. 95.

aggravations of their respective disobedience, rebellion, per-
fidy, and ingratitude.[1]

Swift was not yet an imbecile when he wrote that.

Another document, well-known but not published, is an
account of cathedral collections, kept by Swift privately and
in his own hand. Even a few extracts will give one a taste
of the innumerable quiet charities which underlay Swift's
bitterness concerning Ireland:

Janr. 7 [1740]	A cruel frost of twelve days, and still going. The collections this day were but 2s. 1d., but I added my usuall shilling on common Sundays	0 – 3 – 2
[May 1741]	Given to an honest man one Luke. 10 shillings: of collections and 10 shillings more of my own: in all	1 – 0 – 0
July 23. 1741	Given at the request of Mrs Ridgeway to a poor family in my liberty	0 – 3 – 3
Sept. 27. [1741]	No collection in the church, but I gave	0 – 2 – 8½

18 April 1742 is the terminal date.[2] Swift, then almost
seventy-five, had little more than three years to live. It thus
appears, as an eminent physician, W. R. Wilde, said more
than a century ago, 'Up to the year 1742 Swift showed no
symptom whatever of mental disease, beyond the ordinary
decay of nature.'[3]

Then what happened? When nearly seventy-five, he went

[1] Ball, VI, 220.
[2] MS. in the Victoria and Albert Museum (Forster Collection, item 513,
48. D. 34/9), ff. (inverted) 11, 9v, 10v, 8v, 8.
[3] The Closing Years of Dean Swift's Life (Dublin, 1849), pp. 71-72.

into the sort of decline that a brain lesion, associated with cerebral arteriosclerosis, can produce. He suddenly had great and quickly increasing difficulty expressing himself or understanding others. Swift had by this time been so long withdrawn from normal social life that the new turn remained generally unremarked until an unfortunate incident during the summer of 1742. An inquiry made in July led to a general investigation, the next month, which established that he had, since May, been unable to take care 'either of his estate or person'.[1]

For the remaining years of his life, Swift was protected by a committee of guardians. To set up such a committee, it was legally necessary for there to be a declaration of his lunacy. But this form by no means equals a diagnosis. It was the most convenient way for a senile person, living alone, to be defended against various sorts of exploitation. The investigations and reports were made by Swift's friends and certain other public-spirited citizens; and they had to find him incompetent – for whatever cause – before they could take charge of his affairs.

If we wish to look into Swift's condition during the period which remained, we must try elsewhere; for first-hand reports are not lacking. During his three final years, Swift hardly talked. In October 1742, occurred the orbital cellulitis already described. Otherwise, he speedily reached the state of either keeping silent or uttering a few, rare, disconnected exclamations. But he did not speak nonsense or act wild. Sir Walter Russell Brain has made an unqualified diagnosis of these symptoms: motor aphasia, inability to speak, usually joined with some inability to understand

[1] Ball, VI, 184.

speech. It was precipitated, says Sir Walter, by a brain lesion probably tied up in some way with the orbital cellulitis. In medical language,

> Thrombophlebitis of the superior petrosal sinus is likely to lead to phlebitis of the cortical veins draining the lower part of the frontal lobe, including, on the left side, Broca's area. [This . . .] infective intracranial complication of [Swift's] orbital cellulitis [led] . . . to severe and lasting motor aphasia.[1]

All authorities are agreed that motor aphasia has nothing to do with psychosis, madness, insanity, or imbecility. People in this state can often, like Swift, make emotional exclamations but not propositional statements. Yet the catastrophic forgetfulness, the deafness and dizziness of Ménière's disease, and the general incapacities of his old age set him in a bleak and hideous role. He may have been faintly conscious, again and again, of messages which he could not formulate. When he had begun to withdraw, in the late 1730's, from the circle of approximately his social equals, one incentive to retreat was the dread of humiliating himself before them by some grotesque fit – the incentive which had moved him to leave Pope's home in 1727. After he was seventy-five and speechlessness had broken even his communication with relatives and servants, he was perhaps not spared the bitterness of sensing that they thought him imbecilic at just the moment when intelligence drove him to reach them through words. The sight of Mrs Whiteway when he could not greet her by name shook him so heavily that she was forced to leave and to watch him only in secret. What should dull the pain is our knowledge that Swift preferred consciousness, however stunted, to calm idiocy.

[1] Brain, p. 342.

Johnson, Scott, Thackeray, and Huxley? Masters of language they are, but their understanding of Swift's character is as shallow as their sympathy with him. Swift, from birth to death, was insane by no medical definition. He was no more eccentric or neurotic than Pope or Johnson, and probably less so. The tradition of his madness has been rejected for forty years by every qualified scholar who has bothered to look into the question. For a hundred years the medical experts have cleared him. Why then does the tradition endure?

It is easy to account for the origin of this myth. Swift had always acted with a freedom which gave him the reputation of an eccentric; he also possessed many enemies; he passed the five last years of his life in steadily growing seclusion. The lunacy inquiry, the privately circulated story of the orbital cellulitis delirium and some other events made enough material to engender rumours like that already quoted from Charles Yorke; and the source of Yorke's gossip has significance. He and his brothers received much of their education from Dr Thomas Birch, whom their father patronized. To this scholar, a compulsive and often careless retailer of literary tattle, Horace Walpole gave the character of 'running about like a young setting dog in quest of anything, new or old, and with no parts, taste, or judgment'.[1] In September 1744, Birch, who maintained a long-lived correspondence with Charles Yorke, sent him an obviously fantastic story:

> Dr Swift has lately awak'd from a mere animal life into a thorough misanthropy and brutality of lust; for he can hardly be restrain'd from knocking every man on the head, who

[1] Walpole, *Correspondence* (Yale Edition, New Haven, 1939), II, 186.

comes near him, merely because he is a man, or a *Yahoo*, as he calls him in Gulliver; or from attempting every woman, that he sees. I doubt these were always the real dispositions of him; but now it happens, that the thin disguise, which before scarce cover'd them, is absolutely fallen off.[1]

I believe Birch to be the spring of the earlier tale as well. Since he detested Swift (whom he did not know), was a friend of Johnson's, and supplied materials for the *Lives of the Poets*, and since Johnson himself disliked Swift, it is not surprising that the legend struck deep roots. Though this element is only a small factor in the great myth, its fragility is typical of the traditions associated with Swift's supposed madness.

[1] B.M., Ad. MS. 35396, f. 250. For this reference I am indebted to the erudition and generosity of Mr Edward Ruhe, of Cornell University.

Chapter Seven

OLD AGE

I

In 1745, at the age of seventy-eight, Swift died. He was laid out in his own hall, and the people of Dublin crowded to see him. The coffin stood open; he wore neither cap nor wig. On the front and dome of his skull, little hair remained; but it grew thick behind, resting like white flax on the pillow. The woman who had nursed him sat at his head. When she left the room for a brief time, someone cut off a lock of the hair, which she missed on her return; and after that no person was admitted to see him. Finally, at midnight, three days after his death, Swift was, as he had wished, buried with the utmost privacy on the south side of the great middle aisle of St Patrick's Cathedral.[1]

But the end of his life stopped none of the mouths which had maligned him; for the legend of a daemonic Swift was already passing into this world from the crooked inventions of remote tattlers. It was without effect that his friends denied the fictions; and Johnson's verse made a lapidary inscription of a myth – 'Swift expires a driv'ler and a show.'[2] Although

---

[1] William Monck Mason, *The History and Antiquities of the . . . Church of St Patrick* (Dublin, 1820), pp. 411-12 and note r.

[2] 'The Vanity of Human Wishes', line 318. As early as 1749, Dr John Lyon, the clergyman who had been officially responsible for Swift during the years of incompetence, denied the story of the dean's being shown for money by his

most of the first-hand accounts of Swift's last years have by now been printed, no biographer has yet assembled them all. Hoping that two centuries of scandal and error have not fatally embedded themselves in literary history, I have tried to make a coherent narrative out of the facts preserved by those witnesses who did see Swift during this twilight era. Where the reporters are in conflict, I have both indicated what their original statements were, and offered an interpretation of my own.

II

In July 1739, Swift appointed John Wynne as subdean of the cathedral, because the dean was often (as he himself wrote) 'not able by reason of sickness to be present and personally to preside in the chapter'. Although until March 1742, the cathedral clergy sometimes met in the deanery – rather than the chapter house – so Swift might join them, he had, for practical purposes, ceased to be dean.[1] As his disabilities worked on him, he became more and more of a still centre around which turned, ephemerally, those who wished to reach clerical power through his offices, to win literary distinction through their connection with him, or to protect him from such exploitations. Among the less admirable of the circle was John Boyle, fifth Earl of Orrery.

In 1732, when his father died, this young man, then twenty-four years old, succeeded to the title. The deceased earl had, as an undergraduate at Christ Church, been the pivot of the Phalaris controversy; he had known Swift well

servants (B.M., MS. Ad. 35397, f. 266v). For this reference, I am again indebted to Mr Edward Ruhe.

[1] Landa, *Swift and the Church of Ireland*, p. 95.

in both kingdoms; and they had met for the last time during a flying trip of the earl to Ireland the month before his death. The son arrived a year later, to bring order into a mismanaged estate; but almost immediately he suffered the loss of his wife. It was soon after her death that Swift began to see him. (He remarried in 1738.)

The fourth earl had described this heir as lacking 'taste or inclination, either for the entertainment or knowledge which study and learning afford'. Trying with indifferent resources to refute that judgment, the son achieved a 'feeble-minded' bathos later described by Johnson:

> His conversation was ... neat and elegant, but without strength. He grasped at more than his abilities could reach; tried to pass for a better talker, a better writer, and a better thinker than he was.

Orrery spent his life, said Johnson, in 'catching at' the literary eminence which 'he had not power to grasp'.[1] What he lacked in talent, however, he made up in obsequiousness; and having either patronized or made the acquaintance of a chain of authors from Thomas Southerne to the Rambler, he did at last win a reflected immortality.

When exercised on Swift, Orrery's 'politeness carried to a ridiculous excess' (– Johnson again –) produced the desired attention. 'I meet him sometimes at dinners,' the dean said in October 1732, 'and he hath dined with me. He seems an honest man, and of good dispositions' – alluding as much, probably, to the young peer's Tory politics as to his character. Eight weeks' acquaintanceship drew more praise than insight from Swift: 'I often see Lord Orrery,' he said in

---

[1] Boswell's *Johnson* (Hill-Powell ed., Oxford, 1934-50), V, 238 and note 5; II, 129.

December, 'who seems every way a most deserving person, a good scholar, with much wit, manners and modesty.'[1]

There are many signs of the intimacy which speedily established itself between them. In the spring of 1733, Swift saw to it that a boy recommended by the earl was admitted to the Blue Coats Hospital. The following month, Orrery gave a portrait of his deceased wife to the dean. Within the next few days, we find Swift affectionately refusing first Orrery's loan of a coach and then his present of an expensive snuffbox. They went on outings together, and each saved the other's letters. No doubt, the earl, rejected by his own father, and generally attracted to elderly gentlemen, felt eager to indulge Swift's strong paternal leanings, especially during the lonely months which must have succeeded Orrery's bereavement upon the death of his countess.

Five years of assiduity, including several residences by Orrery in Dublin, attached the dean to him until the younger man's departure for England in 1737 came to be a miserable prospect for Swift. At the end of March, he wrote to the earl, then in Cork, 'Pray, my lord come to us a month before you leave this kingdom, and dine with me every day on scrape with Mrs Whiteway in my bed-chamber; and then I will (multa gemens) tak[e] an eternall farewell of you.' Orrery answered saying that he would sail from Dublin in June: 'I am now forced to bid you farewell; but hereafter expect my whole life and conversation.' Having reached town, however, he found himself, for at least a fortnight, too busy to call at the deanery; and although he did make a visit on June 2, Swift sent him a note more than a week later:

[1] Johnson, in Boswell, IV, 17; *Letters to Ford*, pp. 142, 144.

... as you have nineteen days of this month left, I hope you do not intend that I am not to see you before you go. . . . You shall, you must see me, because I must never see you more: and yet I hope your hours of leisure [i.e., in England] will afford me a line. . . .

The next day, Orrery replied, 'I will certainly see you very often before I go.' But on the eve of his sailing, early the next month, we find the old dean writing, 'I fear you will not have time to see me, so I must bid you farewell for ever'; and in a second note the same day he remarked, 'I have taken my leave of you by a letter, and your lordship hath done the same with me in the kindness [sic] manner. . . .'[1]

At the opposite extreme from Orrery stood the dean's cousin, Martha Whiteway. Swift's commendations of her, his appeals to her, his care for her, revive in a mild but unflickering light his image of Stella. Swift rarely talked or wrote as he felt about his relatives. To his sister, he was far more generous than he gave out. Though he regularly mentioned the bulk of his family with contempt – 'not a grain of merit among them' – he kept on surprisingly good terms with many of them.[2]

Martha Swift, a few years younger than Vanessa, was the last child of Swift's youngest uncle, Adam. At seventeen she married her first husband, Theophilus Harrison. He was

[1] Most of the material in these two paragraphs comes from letters by Swift which are incomplete in Ball's edition. The MSS. are in the Pierpont Morgan Library (V-11-D, MA 455, a bound volume labelled *Orrery Correspondence*). have drawn on those dated 22 March 1732-3; 16, 17, 20 April; 28 May 1733; 31 March, 11 June, 2 July 1737. Orrery's letters are quoted from Ball, VI, 2, 19. It is quite possible that Swift often did not feel well enough to receive Orrery, or that the earl paid him visits which have not been recorded. (The passages omitted by Ball are printed in the Appendix to M. B. Gold, *Swift's Marriage to Stella*, Cambridge, Mass., 1937.) [2] Ball, V, 170·

a clergyman whose mother had been the widow (and fourth wife) of Swift's eldest uncle, Godwin, and whose father was Dean of Clonmacnoise and a prebendary of St Patrick's. Harrison died in 1714, after they had had two children; and in 1716 she married Edward Whiteway, to whom she bore two sons. In 1732 Mrs Whiteway became a widow again, when her youngest child, John, was only nine.

Swift seems always to have liked and respected her thoroughly. Before Edward Whiteway's death, he seldom met her, but, he told her, 'If you knew what I say of you to others, you would believe it was not want of inclination.' By the spring of 1735, however, he could describe her as the only cousin whom he saw.[1] She had begun to visit him several times a week and to keep his household in order. Being an intelligent and well-educated woman, she soon helped him with his correspondence; and if she cannot be called his secretary, it is because she was something more. As Swift neared seventy, his responsibilities did not grow lighter; but his memory became less and less reliable, and his combined deafness and vertigo seized him as often as ever.

Swift interested himself in her children; and her studious, ascetic first-born, Theophilus, charmed him. When the boy died, two years after graduating from T.C.D., Swift mourned with the mother, and he offered her the deanery as a retreat from the last scenes. Mary, her daughter, turned into one of his many young lady pets. Swift also paid a hundred pounds for John Whiteway's apprenticeship to a surgeon – and very appropriately, since Whiteway became not only one of the great Irish medical men of the eighteenth

[1] Ball, IV, 190; V, 170.

century but also the first Visiting Surgeon of the hospital established by Swift's will.[1]

Mrs Whiteway's son-in-law (and Swift's cousin once removed), Deane Swift, was a year older than Lord Orrery and, in his ties with his great relative, both less ambiguous and more ambivalent than the earl. Jonathan Swift had taken up with the young man around 1733, when Deane Swift was twenty-six (though they had already had a family acquaintance for thirteen years). Eight years earlier, perhaps on the basis of misinformation, Swift had labelled the boy a puppy who had 'so behaved himself, as to forfeit all regard or pity'. But in 1726 he began to advance money against mortgages on Deane Swift's 865-acre property, and by 1733 the total debt amounted to two thousand pounds. The young man began to be a steady caller at the deanery only in 1738, when he was probably sponsored by Mrs Whiteway. In the spring of 1739 cousinly affection climbed to the height of calling him 'the most valuable of any of his family' and introducing him to Pope as decent, modest, a man of taste and scholarship, and a lover of 'liberty'.[2]

Deane Swift married Mrs Whiteway's daughter, Mary (Harrison), in the latter part of 1739. Proud of being allied to the celebrated dean, he could not help expecting some benefit to himself not so much as a result of, but rather in conjunction with his attendance on the sick old man. Instead of a career, though (as he had hoped), his main inheritance was the distinction and advantage of publishing Jonathan Swift's works – many of them originals which descended to him through Mrs Whiteway. The only gifts

[1] Ball, V, 334; Maurice J. Craig, *The Legacy of Swift* (Dublin, 1948), p. 42.
[2] Ball, III, 236; Registry of Deeds, MS. memorials 1726-51-33830, 1733-75-52422; Deane Swift, *Essay*, p. 377; Ball, VI, 126-7.

which he received from his illustrious relative were (in 1738)
an Elzevir Virgil, and some items left by the dean's will.[1]
Yet, according to an unconvincing analysis made in 1741
by Deane Swift himself, the relationship could hardly have
been more influential:

> When I was a boy my mother designed me for the bar and I
> would to God I had never been diverted from so reasonable a
> pursuit, but to my great misfortune the Dean of St Patrick's,
> Dr Swift, took notice of me very young, buoyed up my tender
> mind with notions of a more exalted nature, recommended
> history, poetry, the belles lettres, politicks and a contempt of
> logic to a soul by nature too susceptible of so delightful
> imaginations. Everybody looked upon me as the person for
> whom he proposed somewhat extraordinary, even he himself
> talked of recommending me to persons in station who by
> degrees would hand me up the stairs of fortune in the Court
> of St James's.

Not only did these prospects evaporate with no residue,
but the dean seemed actually to shake him off. When Deane
Swift was twenty-three, he began to study divinity and was
recommended to several bishops. To improve his oppor-
tunities, he went to take a degree at Oxford. However, 'I no
sooner thought of going into the church than the dean
pursued me with bitterness' against the plan, which the
younger man, as it happened, abandoned for conscientious
reasons of his own; and a new relationship followed:

> Since I left Oxford and gave over all thoughts of the church
> the dean has been again acquainted with me; I have frequently
> visited him and since I was marryd if I had consented to
> sacrifice my life to him and spend all my days in his house to
> entertain him in his retirement when everybody whom he had

[1] Deane Swift, *Essay*, pp. 353-4.

obliged except one person [i.e., Mrs Whiteway] had absolutely quitted him, then indeed he would have condescended to think he had obliged me by permitting me to keep him company. But anything is better than such slavery and though I have always loved him as a father, yet I could not bear with such treatment and neglect as I had formerly received from him.

The dean's compliments about his scholarship, politics, and virtues meant nothing:

I went so far one night as to ask him very gravely if he knew e'er a young nobleman who wanted Greek and Latin for that I would sell him a bargain of them: he asked me what I meant. I told him that I had spent a great part of my life in the pursuit of ancient learning and that at last I found it was of no use and that if any young lord would purchase it I would sell him all that I was worth in that sort together with all my books in those languages and all the taste I had in poetry for so small a sum as £200, for that I really had no occasion for any of them, and that I should be very glad to get fairly rid of them. He seemed to dislike what I said prodigiously which had no further effect on me than to insist upon the reasonableness of my proposal: he soon talked to a third person and changed the discourse. . . . I have made it my business to drop him by degrees and of late [July 1741] it hath come to that pass that I have seen him but once since the middle of May, and perhaps shall never see him ten times during his life. . . . I admire him as a genius, you know how often I have fought his battels at Oxford, I believe you saw I loved him which, however great a fool soever I am for it, I cannot yet prevail upon myself to repent of . . . I cannot yet wholly get the better of my affection for him.[1]

There are inconsistencies and omissions in this account; yet

[1] Lilian Dickins and Mary Stanton (edd.), *An Eighteenth-Century Correspondence* (London, 1910), pp. 37-40.

the conflict of motives which is quite visible bears out Patrick Delany's second-hand description of Deane Swift: 'a man of fire, a little wild and sufficiently irritable'.[1] His facts are more reliable than his interpretations. Even in this picture, concentrating on his dealings with the great man of his family, he passes over the tremendous loan of £2,000. Elsewhere, Deane Swift's apparent respect for Orrery does not suggest a very deep penetration into human character.

Dr Delany, a friend since 1719 – and one of the most dignified and prosperous of the dean's acquaintances – had stopped seeing Jonathan Swift around the time when Deane Swift's intimacy bloomed; and he evidently supposed that the new habitué's influence had turned the dean against him. But Orrery managed to pile up epistolary records of his passionate devotion to Swift – all very proper to shine in print – without finding an occasion to visit him after about 1738. In December 1740, the earl wrote asking Swift to place a candidate of Orrerys' in the cathedral choir; in January, he pleaded with Mrs Whiteway to bring the ailing dean to Caledon, the Orrerys' country estate (on the eve of the Orrerys' departure for England!):

> His health is extremely dear to me. Would to God you could persuade him to come to Caledon, where Lady Orrery would take care to make the place as agreeable as she could to him and you.

In February he passed through Dublin without seeing Swift; in March he urged the dean to visit Pope and himself in England.[2]

Swift was still far from dead. When he was only fifty-one,

---

[1] *A Letter to Deane Swift* (London, 1755), p. 13.
[2] Ball, VI, 173–5 and note.

he had complained that his eyes began to 'grudge' him reading. Seven years later he said he could read neither small print nor 'anything by candlelight'.[1] As his eyesight grew weaker, he read less and less because he refused to wear spectacles; and so he spent more time in physical exercise. He found himself often disabled by one or another of his varied afflictions. Throughout 1741, however, he could carry on a number of duties: keeping certain cathedral accounts in his own hand (until April 1742), writing a letter of recommendation, attending cathedral chapters. Deane Swift's remarks during the summer of 1741 suggest that the dean was still quite competent. It was in 1742 that his decline suddenly speeded up, perhaps with a push from some otherwise unnoticed brain strokes.

II

Few men touched Swift as Addison and Arbuthnot did – drawing forth his liveliest conversation, setting him at ease without weakening their own dignity or Swift's, holding his respect as well as his love. These were the ripest of his masculine friendships; Delany is one of the last if not the dimmest of this tradition. However, what the ageing Swift wanted like bread was the brother-cum-confidant, whom he need not fear or distrust, and who demanded no reserve – a not contemptible playmate. Charles Ford, the one most precisely designed for that function, settled in England and never saw Swift after 1732. Thomas Sheridan died in 1738. The least attractive of such cronies, and the last in the succession, was Dr Francis Wilson, a sinister and puzzling figure

[1] *Letters to Ford*, p. 72; Ball, III, 236-7.

in Swift's era of decline – the age, as Proust says, 'at which a Victor Hugo chooses to surround himself, above all, with Vacqueries and Meurices'.[1]

In 1727, when Wilson was thirty and Swift sixty, Archbishop King preferred the young priest to the vicarage of Clondalkin, near Dublin, and to the prebend of Kilmactalway in St Patrick's Cathedral. Although Wilson held these livings until his death, he never rose beyond them. In a memoir long afterward, his parish clerk at Clondalkin, Peter Brett, wrote that Wilson had an unparalleled memory and an extraordinary erudition; yet when, having taken his degree at Trinity College, Dublin, he had sat for a fellowship, he failed to win one. Wilson's appearance would have been prepossessing: his proportions were good, he was of average height, and he had a pleasant face. But it was probably his graces that charmed Swift; for the admiring clerk describes him as a cheerful and accommodating person with a gift for fluent, entertaining talk. He had evidently some of the childlike appeal of a courteous and intelligent boy.

For ten years Swift paid little attention to him. But around the time of Sheridan's last illness and death, the dean handed on to Wilson much of the interest and love which he had felt toward the innocent schoolmaster. Toward 1737 he made him tenant of the deanery tithes. The septuagenarian took such pleasure in his company that Wilson began to stay for long periods in the deanery, where a room was kept for him, although he continued to reside at Newlands, his house in Clondalkin. Among Swift's cathedral accounts for May 1739, is a memorandum which both bears out the Clondalkin clerk's praise of his master's charity, and shows

---

[1] *The Captive* (London, 1941), II, 114.

(by its irony) how tender Swift felt toward him; it is a note that Swift had enlarged the weekly sum which he gave to John Lyon for alms to the poor:

> Increased to Mr Lyon, by the pernicious vice and advice of my daily sponge and inmate Will's son, to twelve scoundrels at 6½d. per week, 6s. 6d.[1]

From Swift's intimate use of Wilson's name here and in letters, it is plain that the younger man enjoyed very much the same standing at the deanery as Mrs Whiteway. But Swift's sober friends and relatives suspected Wilson of cheating him out of rent for the deanery tithes and out of the dean's share of the Clondalkin tithes. They claimed that Swift's servants saw Wilson coming in with his portmanteau empty and leaving with it full of books; and there is, in fact, evidence that Wilson did remove books from the deanery, although we may suppose that he borrowed them with Swift's consent and that Swift's friends felt anxious about the dean's own judgment.[2] In his will, Swift left him copies of Plato's works, Clarendon's history, his own 'best bible', thirteen small Persian pictures, and a silver tankard. (It is an irony that Wilson's books came eventually to be auctioned with Swift's.) But in December 1742, Deane Swift wrote that 'so long as the Dean's memory and judgment were tolerable, Wilson seldom or never paid the Dean any money but in the presence of Mrs Whiteway, and after the Dean's memory failed, he always paid the Dean in private; notwithstanding he was frequently warned to the contrary.'[3]

[1] On Peter Brett's recollections of Francis Wilson, see E. St John Brooks, 'Swift and Dr Wilson', in the *Times Literary Supplement*, 7 August 1943, p. 379, and 9 October 1943, p. 487; the cathedral accounts are quoted from the MS. (see above, note 2 on p. 122), f. 2.

[2] Sir Harold Williams, *Dean Swift's Library* (Cambridge, 1932), pp. 15-22.

[3] *Times Literary Supplement*, 24 May 1934, p. 376.

It seems more than a coincidence that Swift had little to do with Delany after Wilson had grown into a frequenter of the deanery. The staid and rather humourless Dean of Down must have classed Wilson among those who desired, 'by all the evil arts of insinuation and untruth, to banish the Dean's best friends from about him, and make a monopoly of him to themselves . . . for what ends, they best know.'[1] Whether the 'best friends' felt ready to provide Swift's ego with the ungartered fellowship which was its elementary food, Delany does not say. But Wilson was one of two witnesses of Swift's last official document, a complaint which seems in part directed against the subdean, John Wynne, whom Wilson allegedly wished to replace.

This 'exhortation' is dated 28 January 1742; two drafts are preserved, of which the first is the more elaborate and intemperate. Its purpose was to forbid the singers and musicians of the cathedral to 'assist at a club of fiddlers in Fishamble Street', and to have the subdean execute punishments appropriate to the degree of their offence. From the many invocations of the subdean, and from an expression of Swift's anxiety 'to preserve the dignity of my station', I suspect Wilson of egging the old dean on to believe that Wynne had behaved with improper lenience. Perhaps the vicar of Clondalkin possessed the assurance to suppose that if he brought Swift to place him in Wynne's office, the chapter would accept the appointment.[2]

Four and a half months after the exhortation, on the morning of 14 June 1742, Wilson came to the deanery. There are several authorities for what followed: the affidavit

---

[1] Delany, *Observations upon Lord Orrery's Remarks*, p. 3.
[2] Ball, VI, 220-1.

of Swift's servant, Richard Brennan, delivered to John Rochfort on 16 June; Wilson's sworn statement on 13 July; and the account gathered by Deane Swift and written down half a year after the event.[1] Wilson said that Swift received him with 'his usual fondness, which was always very great'. The dean told Wilson that 'he would take the air that morning, and dine with him at his house in the country'. Wilson said he called for the dean's coach and for Mrs Ridgeway (the housekeeper), but the coachman and she were both away; so a hackney 'was sent for'. Deane Swift insists that Wilson hurried 'the dean out of town in a hackney coach, without taking his friend Mrs Ridgeway along with him, which the dean has always done, ever since he began to be conscious of his want of memory, and other infirmities.'

Brennan, Swift's servant, said only that 'some short time' after Wilson went in to Swift, a hackney coach was called by Wilson's directions; and as soon as the coach came to the entrance of the deanery, Wilson put Swift into it. After telling Brennan to take Wilson's mare and follow them, he 'immediately order'd the coachman to drive to Newland', his residence. In less than an hour (that is, as soon as he could get ready), Brennan followed, on Wilson's mare. He overtook them on the road. With Swift's friends displaying in advance so much distrust of Wilson, the tradition easily established itself that he deliberately lured Swift to Newlands when no responsible person could protect the old man; Mrs Ridgeway's comment does not appear.

[1] For these accounts, see Maxwell B. Gold, 'The Brennan Affidavit', *Times Literary Supplement*, 17 May 1934, p. 360; Sir Harold Williams, 'The Brennan Affidavit', ibid., 24 May 1934, p. 376 (Deane Swift's letter); and Ball, VI, 179-81 (Wilson's affidavit).

Deane Swift writes that Brennan reported one circumstance which Swift's friends would not circulate in the affidavit: that Wilson got the dean drunk:

> Now the dean's stint for about half a year before, was two larger bumpers of wine somewhat more than half a pint. When the dean had drunk this quantity, Wilson pressed him to another glass, which the dean's footman observing, told Wilson, in a low voice, that his master never drank above two glasses, and that if he forced him to drink a third, it would certainly affect his head. But Wilson not only made light of this caution, and imposed another glass upon the dean, but called afterwards for a bottle of strong white wine, and forced the dean to drink of it, which in a short time, did so intoxicate him, that he was not able to walk to the coach without being supported: and after all this, Wilson called at an ale house on his way to Dublin, and forced the poor dean to swallow a dram of brandy.

After dinner, between five and six in the evening, they started back to Dublin, with Brennan riding behind the coach. Along the way, Brennan said, he heard Wilson ask Swift to make him subdean; Wilson abused Wynne as a 'stupid fellow, which I am not'. Swift refused and asked for his money (perhaps meaning arrears of the deanery tithes of Clondalkin). Wilson said, 'Sir, I am paying you your money and will pay you.' After a few minutes, Wilson began to curse, saying several times, 'By God no man shall strike me, and if King George wou'd strike me, I would cut his throat.' While he was swearing, they came near Kilmainham, and Wilson shouted to the coachman, 'You villain, you rascal, stop the coach.' Brennan jumped from behind and opened the door to let Wilson out. When the prebendary had stepped down, he turned about and said to Swift, 'You are a stupid old blockhead, and an old rascal, and only you are too old, I would beat you, and God damn me but I will cut your throat.' Brennan tried 'all in his power' to get the door shut; and when he had done so, he told the coachman to drive to the deanery, whereupon Wilson said, 'God damn him, drive away the old stupid blockhead.'

Wilson's account has little in common with Brennan's. He said Swift drank half a pint of white wine at dinner, and for two miles of the way back treated Wilson most affectionately. But suddenly he cried out that Wilson was the devil and told him to go to hell, repeating these words 'in a most astonishing rage'. Wilson took no notice and tried to appease him by reciting some passages 'out of such authors as the dean admired most'. Instead of listening, Swift struck him several times on the face, 'scratched him, and tore off his wig'. Wilson, out of pity, did not oppose Swift until he shoved his fingers into the other's eyes. Then Wilson 'ordered the coach to stop, which he left with the natural expressions of resentment and indignation, declaring he would not again tamely suffer the greatest man on earth to strike him.'

Deane Swift reports that the dean had one arm black and blue the next morning, but admits that 'whether [Wilson] struck the dean or not is uncertain'. This detail can be reconciled with the rest if we suppose that Wilson did urge Swift to make him subdean, that the irritable old man got angry and made gestures of hitting him, that Wilson – to defend himself – held Swift's arm tightly enough to bruise it while, to soothe the dean's indignation, he recited passages from Swift's favourite reading, and that when he could not restrain Swift, Wilson – perhaps not wholly sober – grew furious himself and got out of the coach. Swift is reported to have asked for Wilson as soon as he came home, saying, 'Where is Dr Wilson? Ought not the Doctor to be here this afternoon?'[1] But Wilson seems never to have entered the deanery again.

III

While the evidence did not warrant judicial proceedings, and Wilson retained his vicarage and his prebend, those who were attached to Swift felt thoroughly alarmed. 'It was the talk of the town,' said Deane Swift, 'that a statute of lunacy ought to be taken out, in order to guard the dean against further insults, and wrongs of all kinds.' A preliminary inquiry was ordered, which was carried out in July, not to investigate Swift's sanity (he was never insane by modern definitions) but rather as a move in the direction of overseeing his person and his affairs. Little transpired to exculpate Wilson or to lighten the pathos of Swift's wretchedness. A general investigation, the next month, into Swift's condition ended all doubt as to his needs:

> [He] hath for these nine months past, been gradually failing in his memory and understanding, and [is] of such unsound mind and memory that he is incapable of transacting any business, or managing, conducting, or taking care either of his estate or person.

20 May 1742 was given as the date after which he was irresponsible; and for the remaining years of his life he was protected by a committee of guardians.[2]

Very soon after the committee was appointed, Deane

---

[1] *Times Literary Supplement*, 24 May 1934, p. 376.　　[2] Ball, VI, 181-5.

Swift went into the invalid's dining-room and found him walking there. The visitor said something casual; and the old dean, instead of making any answer, first pointed with his hand to the door, saying, 'Go, go,' and then at once raised his hand to his head with the words, 'My best understanding.' Breaking off abruptly, he walked away.

Mrs Whiteway was the last person he could name. When that memory failed, he grew (for a time) so uncontrollable at meeting any caller that he could not rest for a night or two afterwards. So she was forced to leave him and could only come by twice a week to ask about his health and to see that proper care was taken of him. Fearing to upset him, she would not look at him unless his back was towards her.

In October 1742 his left eye was inflamed and the lid so much discoloured that John Nichols, the surgeon, expected it to mortify; boils appeared on Swift's arms and body; he was in torment. For a week it took three people to hold him when he tried to tear off the bandage; and for nearly a month he hardly slept two hours out of the twenty-four. Yet he continued to have a fair appetite.

The last day of this illness, he took Mrs Whiteway's hand and called her by name, showing his usual pleasure in seeing her. She asked him whether he would give her dinner. 'To be sure,' he said, 'my old friend.' That day he knew the doctor, the surgeon, and all his family so well that Nichols thought he might regain enough of his understanding to call for what he wanted and to stand some old friends' visits for amusement. But the day or two after the pain was gone brought a relapse. Free from agony, his eye almost well, he became very quiet and began to sleep, but could hardly be brought to walk a turn about his room.

For the three years of life which remained to him, Swift spoke little. There was a servant to shave his cheeks and all his face as low as the tip of his chin once a week; but when the hair grew long under the chin and about the throat, it was cut with scissors. His meat was served up ready cut, and sometimes he would let it lie on the table an hour before he would touch it, and then eat it walking. If the servant stayed in the room, he would not eat or drink; and he walked a great deal, sometimes ten hours a day. Sometimes he would say nothing, sometimes incoherent words: he never talked nonsense or said a foolish thing. On the morning of his birthday in 1743, Mrs Ridgeway reminded him of the occasion and said that people were getting ready to celebrate it with bonfires and illuminations. 'It is all folly,' said Swift. 'They had better let it alone.' Once, early in 1744, he seemed to wish to talk to Deane Swift, who had come to see him. In order to try what the poor old man would say, the visitor announced that he was staying for dinner. 'Won't you give Mr Swift a glass of wine, Sir?' asked Mrs Ridgeway. The dean shrugged his shoulders, just as he used to do when he did not want a friend to spend the evening with him – as much as to say, 'You'll ruin me in wine.' Again he tried, with a good deal of pain, to find words; at last, after many attempts, he gave a heavy sigh. Another time, the servant was breaking up a large, stubborn piece of coal. 'That's a stone, you blockhead,' said Swift. Another day, as Swift's watch was lying on the table, the servant picked it up to find out the time; Swift said, 'Bring it here.' When it was shown to him, he looked very attentively at it.

One day in mid-March 1744, as Swift sat in his chair, he reached toward a knife, but Mrs Ridgeway moved it away from him. He shrugged his shoulders, rocked himself, and said, 'I am what I am, I am what I am'; some minutes later he repeated the same thing two or three times. About a fortnight afterwards, he tried to speak to his servant, whom he sometimes called by name. Not finding words to tell what he meant, he showed some uneasiness and said, 'I am a fool' – his last recorded words.[1]

[1] Ball, VI, 185-90. In a few details I have departed from these accounts and followed Dr Lyon's notes (see above, note 3 on p. 39).

APPENDIX

Further study persuaded me that sections iv and v of my discussion of *Gulliver's Travels* were misleading. So I venture to reprint the following article as a corrective. It originally appeared in the *Review of English Literature,* Vol. III (July, 1962), pp. 18-38.

The Meaning of Gulliver's Last Voyage

I<small>F</small> a man consistently lies to those who have reason to trust him, he is a bad man.[1] We may soften this judgement in the face of mitigating evidence—that he is two years old, that he is a paranoid schizophrenic, and so forth; but if he is otherwise normal, such mendacity marks him as wicked. At the same time, however, we do not conceive of the normal man as wicked: a true man, 'a real man', is implicitly classed as good. In other words, we do think of a normal man as one who would rather speak the truth than lie. Thus, zoology apart, we carry around a definition according to which we not only distinguish but judge ourselves, and not as a sort of animal but as men.

Knowing ourselves closely, we find mitigating evidence for most of our departures from the definition; and having pardoned ourselves, we likewise and willingly excuse those we love. Indeed,

[1] In these quotations neither the italics nor the capitals of the original texts have been followed except where they have their modern significance. The account given of Part IV of *Gulliver* in this essay will be found to differ fundamentally from that given by me in earlier studies (*PMLA*, LXXII, 1957, pp. 889–95; *The Personality of Jonathan Swift,* 1958, pp. 99–109). In writing this essay, I have drawn heavily upon several sources: an unpublished lecture by Professor R. S. Crane; George Sherburn, 'Errors concerning the Houyhnhnms', *Modern Philology,* LVI, 1958, pp. 92–7; L. A. Landa, a review of my *Personality of Swift* in *Philological Quarterly,* XXXVIII, 1959, pp. 351–3; R. L. Colie, 'Gulliver, the Locke-Stillingfleet Controversy, and the Nature of Man', *History of Ideas News Letter* (New York), II, 1956, pp. 58–62; O. W. Ferguson, 'Swift's *Saeva Indignatio* and *A Modest Proposal*', *Philological Quarterly,* XXXVIII, 1959, pp. 473–9; Stuart Hampshire, 'Criticism and Regret', in *Thought and Action,* 1959. Mr. Hampshire's phrases are sometimes echoed in my sections I and V. I am indebted to Miss Kathleen Williams of University College, Cardiff, and to Mr. Alastair Fowler of Brasenose College, Oxford, for several references used in section II. (After this article went to press, Professor Crane's lecture was published, in somewhat altered form, as 'The Houyhnhnms, the Yahoos, and the History of Ideas', in *Reason and the Imagination,* ed. J. A. Mazzeo, 1962, pp. 231–53.)

the art of excusing becomes in most people so refined that they end by fencing off the original definition in order that they may act with little regard for it. The definition meanwhile remains both static and intact, always available for exhibition, though, to be sure, if the individual gladly acknowledges it, common behaviour regularly insults it. Through this familiar routine, morality as a form of exploratory self-criticism is painlessly dissolved.

The problem of a moralist like Swift is less to re-define man in terms of new ideals than to knock down the fences around an accepted definition, compelling men both to measure themselves by this and to re-examine it. Now in regard to the general problem of making a definition, it is a commonplace that all classifications of concepts depend upon a single essence or a list of essential properties, and furthermore that the choice of such properties can be tested by the analysis of critical examples of the concept being defined. Thus in either choosing an essence or drawing up a list for the concept *man*, we may ask, concerning each proposed property, whether or not such and such an odd or doubtful example possesses it, or else whether or not some indubitable example lacks it. So we may wonder, Is an infant a real man? Is an idiot? An embryo? A corpse? Or we may ask, Did Socrates betray his compatriots? Did he try to preserve his children? Did he live rationally? Often we go further and manufacture unreal and even fantastic examples in order to test the criteria of *man* and thereby to separate essential from superficial qualities. If a moralist can lure people into making such tests, he can by this means force them to recognise their lack of the very properties by which they pretend to define themselves.

When the process operates the other way, from case to definition, the critical example which Swift or any moralist produces may drive an intelligent reader to make deep changes in a hitherto half-conscious conceptual scheme. Merely through being asked how his classification of human qualities would stand up in circumstances not previously envisaged—for Ugolino in the tower, or for St. Paul at the moment of conversion—a person may come to decide that powers or activities which had seemed to belong together should in fact be arranged under separate headings, that what had seemed to him divine was in fact human, and that what had seemed peculiarly a part of *man* really belonged to certain lower animals.

To such discriminations many attributes or actions which ordinarily appear human are irrelevant: an ape may wear our clothing, a bird may parrot our sounds, a dolphin may learn our games, and a young orang-utang may look and act like some human babies. Yet in ordinary affairs we take the superficial token for the thing, giving to each being the benefit of his signs; for what looks like a man dressed in our clothes, speaking our words and playing our games, we start by treating as we would a real man, a normal man, a good man, even though experience and reflection may reveal him to be a criminal or a fool. And should one pursue these reflections far enough, turning them upon the unmitigated experience of one's own inexcusable conduct, one may even come—regretfully, I hope—to the paradoxical conclusion that none of the virtues essential to men are within one's particular reach. To arrive at that conclusion for any individual is still to impugn neither the separate virtues nor the definition. After all, no triangle is a perfect triangle, and the idea of health is genuine although nobody is wholly healthy. So *man* may be a valid concept though men never quite (and some men never at all) fit it; and we may therefore test its validity by applying it to borderline cases. In accordance with this line of reasoning we might as one possibility conclude that a person is human if he is in the class of creatures who both could turn into good men and try to do so.

The comical satirist differs from other moralists in that he does not argue in favour of the common definition. Rather he brings it dramatically to bear upon critical examples, startling the reader into an act of choice which he has hitherto avoided, viz. between the concept and the case. Suddenly the reader is confronted with the need either to surrender a sound definition or to strip a label from an unsound case. And this is the scheme of *A Modest Proposal*.

Swift makes no attempt, in the satire, to deny the validity of the conventional idea of a normal (and therefore good) man. Rather he invokes it by implication.

As it happens, Locke had minutely examined such problems of classification and definition when he attacked the doctrine of innate ideas. For example, in the course of his attack Locke tried to prove that no moral, or 'practical', rules can be innate; and for this purpose he selected several rules which appear incontrovertibly valid, universally self-evident, or, as I should say, which appear of so fundamental an order as to identify men as human: e.g. that one should do as he would be done unto, or that men should keep their compacts, or that parents should preserve their children. Locke then proceeded to show that communities and situations existed in which each of these rules was violated:

It is familiar among the Mingrelians, a people professing Christianity, to bury their children alive without scruple. There are places where they eat their own children. The Caribbees were wont to geld their children, on purpose to fat and eat them. And Garcilasso de la Vega tells us of a people in Peru which were wont to fat and eat the children they got on their female captives, whom they kept as concubines for that purpose, and when they were past breeding, the mothers themselves were killed too and eaten.[1]

The strength of Locke's argument depends not upon the doubtfulness of the maxim being judged but rather upon its authority. Each is a supreme law of human conduct although some people break it. 'If any [moral principle] can be thought to be naturally imprinted, none, I think, can have a fairer pretence to be innate than this: "Parents, preserve and cherish your children" ' (I. ii. 12). The argument works *a fortiori*: if the most powerful, most basic moral principles can be ignored, then none can be innate.

Now we may turn Locke's implications inside out and say that when such a rule is broken, the violators mark themselves as not human. If we wish to trace the ramifications yet further, we may add that to assume that people will violate such a rule is to regard them as beasts. And this is what I believe Swift said in *A Modest*

---

[1] *Essay concerning Human Understanding*, Bk. I, chap. ii, par. 9; ed. A. C. Fraser (Oxford, 1894), I, p. 73.

Proposal. He invoked a definition which he knew the Irish reader accepted, viz. that it is the nature of men to love their children. Next he introduced an implicit minor premise, viz. that the Irish are not to be regarded as men. Finally, he drew his conclusion, that nobody in Ireland would object to the butchering of children for the table.

The essential device in the satire is to lure the Irish reader into identifying himself with the writer. The kindly tone of the opening paragraph, the public spirit of the second, and the businesslike confidence of the third achieve this seduction. 'The author and I have the same nature', says the reader—whereupon Swift replies, 'You have indeed', and springs his trap. In repudiating the rest of the essay, the Irish reader must acknowledge either that his definition of man is not valid or else that his treatment of his own humble compatriots (and their indifference to such treatment) is inhuman; for three bad harvests had revealed that the sight of starving mankind affected Irish landlords as little as the sight of a slaughtered pig.[1]

II

Through the satire of *A Modest Proposal*, then, Swift takes an accepted definition of man and draws the reader into testing an example by it. The result of course should be to shock the reader into rejecting the example. Through the satire of the last part of *Gulliver's Travels*, on the other hand, Swift takes some fantastic examples of real or apparent humanity and has us test accepted definitions by them. The result this time should be to drive the reader to revise his own concepts. The object satirised is now broader, of course, than it was to become in *A Modest Proposal*; for not merely the Irish nor their landlords but rather men as such are being reproached. Similarly, the accusation presented is more general. In my terms it may be expressed as a complaint that while men talk of themselves according to one definition, they

[1] For my assumption that *A Modest Proposal* is primarily addressed to an Irish audience, see Ferguson.

not only act according to another—which happens to conflict with the first—but ought in fact to adopt a third. To put it at first somewhat briefly, when men talk of themselves, they use the description 'rational creatures'. When they deal with one another, however, they rely upon superficial and external criteria such as shape and clothing. Yet the truth is that the first standard is impossible and the second is absurd. A real, normal, true man is one who tries to be rational. I should like to explore the implications of these ideas by way of an extensive diversion, mainly again through some remarks of John Locke, after which I shall return to the route of Gulliver's final voyage.

Professor Ronald S. Crane has shown convincingly that throughout this voyage Swift is playing with the maxims and illustrations found in traditional manuals of logic. Regularly, the compilers of these manuals define man as *animal rationale*. Among their most common examples of *animal irrationale* is *equus*. They also employ such sentences as *Si simia non sit irrationalis, est homo*. In distinguishing between the essential and the accidental properties of our species, the logicians give *vestis* as *composita per accidens*. To underline the importance of such data, one need only remember the role which clothes, simians, and equines play in determining for Gulliver the essential properties of man.[1]

Among these traditional comparisons the man-horse parallel early became a commonplace[2] and could often therefore be invoked ironically, in mock-logic. For instance, Sir Philip Sidney, speaking of a friend who had been attributing high human virtues to horses, says, 'If I had not been a piece of a logician before I came to him, I think he would have persuaded me to have wished myself a horse' (*Defence of Poesy*, par. 2). Similarly, in *Hudibras*, Samuel Butler says his hero would 'undertake to prove by force / Of argument, a man's no horse' (I. i. 71–2); and

[1] Cf. Narcissus Marsh, *Institutiones logicæ* (Dublin, 1681), pp. 184–5 (*equus*), sig. A5 (*simia*), p. 38 (*vestis*), and passim. For these important facts I am indebted to Professor Crane, although my interpretation of them is different from his, and the sentences about *simia* and *vestis* were not used by him.

[2] A well-known ancient example, often imitated, is the conversation between Ulysses and the horse in the *Gryllus* dialogue of Plutarch's *Moralia*.

Hudibras, in a contrast between synods and bears, says, 'That both are *animalia*, / I grant, but not *rationalia*'; Ralpho, he says, can 'no more make bears of these, / Than prove my horse is Socrates' (I. iii. 1277-8, 1281-2).

Furthermore, in serious arguments about the meaning of *individual*, *person*, and *species*, the two elements of the horse-man antithesis tended to be so described as to isolate and dramatise the central issue; for the imaginary horse is most useful in such an argument if he is the most excellent conceivable of his kind; the imaginary man, if he is the most degenerate. Thus the problem of defining the human species becomes that of differentiating a rational, idealised horse from a degenerate, irrational man. Professor Rosalie L. Colie has noticed an extreme instance of this development in the speculations of Anne Conway. To Lady Conway it appeared that metempsychosis and the transmutation of animal species were facts in nature. Yet she insists that such changes do not turn one essential individual into another. She can therefore make up the case of a horse which grows more excellent with each re-birth, coming nearer and nearer the nature and species of a man but retaining its essential individuality. Since, moreover, it is laid down that infinite excellence belongs only to God and Christ, the finite gap between equinity and humanity must be passable, Lady Conway says, and so must the road from man to beast; for since man, 'by his voluntary transgression', has depressed his own nature into a condition as vile in spirit as the most unclean beast, 'what injustice will this be, if God should also compel him to bear that image outwardly in his body, into the which he hath inwardly transformed himself?' [1] Lady Conway is trying to define a human individual so that the concept will be independent of both the rationality and the shape which are associated with the species. She chooses to start from beings who share the former while differing sharply in the latter. But the other combination—identical shape, different reasoning powers—is just as logical, and we shall find it used as well.

---

[1] [Lady Anne Conway] *The Principles of the Most Ancient and Modern Philosophy* (London, 1692), pp. 71-2.

For Swift's generation it was a commonplace that the human body makes an insufficient mark of humanity; apes, monkeys, and monsters were invoked to prove this. Yet certain kinds of reason could also, it seemed, be found in lower animals. While, of course, the ancients were, as Swift knew, familiar with the argument that reason does not belong exclusively to mankind, it is Montaigne in particular who dramatised that argument for the tradition to which *Gulliver's Travels* belongs; and it was he above all whom Descartes intended to refute through the doctrine that animals are automatons devoid of thought. At the same time, the doctrine of animal rationality found so many simple or direct applications among the moral philosophers that some writers employed it ironically or indirectly to satirise human foolishness.[1]

Among these is an acknowledged model for *Gulliver's Travels*, the fantastic voyages of Cyrano de Bergerac. In the moon, Cyrano finds giant men walking on all fours who mistake him for a baboon. There is a long argument as to whether or not he is an irrational animal. In Cyrano's *Histoire des oiseaux* the narrator is captured by intelligent birds. To protect himself from them, Cyrano claims to be a monkey educated and corrupted by men: 'The habits and the food of these dirty beasts [i.e. men]', he says, 'had acquired so much power over me that even my parents, who are monkeys of honour, would hardly recognise me now.' Nevertheless, the birds argue that precisely because he is irrational, he must be a man. 'Since the poor beast has not the use of reason like ourselves', says his partridge prosecutor, 'I excuse his errors in so far as they are produced by lack of understanding.' Cyrano is finally saved by a parrot which had belonged to a cousin and which he had often used as evidence to prove that birds can reason.[2]

[1] See George Boas, *The Happy Beast* (Baltimore, 1933); Elizabeth Barker, 'Giovanni Battista Gelli's *Circe* and Jonathan Swift', *Cesare Barbieri Courier* (Trinity College, Hartford), II, November 1959, pp. 3–15. Miss Barker's parallels between Gelli and Swift are unconvincing, but she does illuminate the traditions to which *Gulliver* belongs.

[2] Cyrano de Bergerac, *Voyages to the Sun and the Moon*, trans. Richard Aldington (London, 1923), pp. 241, 254, 260. Swift's use of Cyrano is considered in detail by W. A. Eddy, in *Gulliver's Travels: A Study in Sources* (Princeton, 1923).

Swift's master, Sir William Temple, was an admirer and imitator of Montaigne; he had read Cyrano; and he inevitably touched on the problem of animal rationality and human shape in essays which we know Swift read. In remarking that various properties have been suggested as peculiar to mankind, Temple lists the most common as reason, shape, speech, laughter, and tears. But critics of vulgar opinion, he points out, have disallowed each of these traits: e.g. the human shape has been found in 'some kind of baboons, or at least such as they call drills'; and human reason, says Temple, is often attributed to such animals as dogs, owls, foxes, elephants, and horses.[1]

Even in our own day both the issue and this approach to it remain interesting, witness the following reflection by Mr. Stuart Hampshire:

If creatures from another planet, anatomically similar to men, were discovered, would we choose to call them men, if they had no language, social conventions and powers of thought and of expression above the animal level? Evidently not. If creatures from another planet, anatomically very unlike men, were discovered, would we choose to call them men, if they communicated thoughts and intentions in a language that we could understand? Evidently the answer would depend on the purposes for which this classification was required. For ordinary practical purposes, and if the interests of physical science were disregarded, we would classify them as men, because we would treat them as we treat human beings in all our ordinary dealings with them. They would play the same, or a sufficiently similar, part in our lives as human beings now play.[2]

III

Of all the parallels with these preoccupations of Swift the most illuminating, I think, are those of John Locke. In the *Essay concerning Human Understanding* Locke had minutely examined the problem of defining the human species. During the course of this examination he made frequent use of two terms, 'real essence' and 'nominal essence'. For Locke the 'real essence' means the true internal constitution of particular substances or ideas; thus what-

---

[1] 'Of Popular Discontents', *Miscellanea. The Third Part* (1701), pp. 1–5.

[2] Hampshire, *Thought and Action*, p. 228.

ever it is which ultimately makes a man a man, is his 'real essence'. Unfortunately, however, we can never directly know the real essence of a substance (such as man), says Locke. Instead, we can only list the perceptible qualities by which in practice we recognise a man, for example, as such; and the idea constituted of these outward, observable qualities, Locke called the 'nominal essence', an abstraction. To demonstrate his lessons, Locke naturally fell back upon the traditional examples; and since he took reason and shape to be the most important properties of the nominal essence, he often paired off men with simians, showing that these two properties were not necessarily tied to one another. Here are a few of his arguments:

There are creatures in the world that have shapes like ours, but are hairy, and want language and reason. There are naturals [i.e. idiots] amongst us that have perfectly our shape, but want reason, and some of them language too. There are creatures as it is said . . . that, with language and reason and a shape in other things agreeing with ours, have hairy tails; others where the males have no beards and the females have. If it be asked whether these be all *men* or no, all of human species? it is plain, the question refers only to the nominal essence. . . . Shall the difference of hair only on the skin be a mark of a different internal specific constitution between a changeling [i.e. an idiot] and a drill [i.e. a baboon], when they agree in shape, and want a reason and speech? [III. vi. 22.]

Among the best-known passages in the *Essay concerning Human Understanding* used to be the anecdote, anticipating Mr. Hampshire's speculation, which Locke relates to support the argument that the word 'man' as popularly, but mistakenly, employed refers to the human shape and not to human faculties. He writes: 'Whoever should see a creature of his own shape or make, though it had no more reason all its life than a cat or a parrot, would call him still a *man*; or whoever should hear a cat or a parrot discourse, reason, and philosophise, would call or think it nothing but a *cat* or a *parrot*; and say, the one was a dull irrational man, and the other a very intelligent rational parrot.' He then tells the anecdote, a supposedly true story of a parrot which could converse like a man. Next, Locke asks whether if this parrot and all of its race had always talked so, they would not have been treated as *rational animals*, yet whether, for all that, they would not still have been classed not as men but as parrots. 'For I presume it is not the idea of a thinking or rational being alone that makes the *idea of a man* in most people's sense: but of a body so and so shaped, joined to it' (II. xxvii. 9–10). One scholar has said that the parrot anecdote must have left a deep impression on everyone who read Locke's *Essay*, and that 'more than one of his professed admirers seemed to recollect little else which they had learned from that work than the story of this parrot' (II. xxvii. 9, n. 2). To Swift the story would have been peculiarly familiar, since he wrote it: I mean literally, 'wrote', because he did not compose it. Locke found the anecdote in Temple's *Memoirs*, and it was Swift who made the copy of the *Memoirs* which was sent to the printer.[1]

As early as *A Tale of a Tub* this question of accident *versus* essence, shape *versus* reason, may have touched Swift. That such preoccupations floated behind the clothes allegories of the *Tale* in general and behind the outside-inside imagery of the *Digression on Madness* in particular, is suggested by some of Locke's remarks:

That all things that have the outward shape and appearance of a man must necessarily be designed to an immortal future being after this life: or, secondly, That whatever is of human birth must be so . . . is to attribute more to the outside than inside of things; and to place the excellency of a man more in the external shape of his body, than internal perfections of his soul: which is but little better than to annex the great and inestimable advantage of immortality and life everlasting . . . to the cut of his beard, or the fashion of his coat. For this or that outward mark of our bodies no more carries with it the hope of an eternal duration, than the fashion of a man's suit gives him reasonable grounds to imagine it will never wear out, or that it will make him immortal [IV. iv. 15; cf. pars. 13, 14, 16].

Although in *Gulliver's Travels* these issues are most deeply considered in the *Voyage to the Houyhnhnms*, Swift alludes to them in Brobdingnag. When the giant king first saw Gulliver, he thought the tiny man might be a piece of clockwork. 'But, when he heard my voice, and found what I delivered to be regular and rational,

[1] See Fraser's note to Locke, I, p. 446; Swift, *Correspondence*, ed. F. E. Ball (1910–14), I, p. 172. Locke added the parrot in his 4th ed., 1700.

he could not conceal his astonishment.' (chap. 3) This may be an allusion to one of Descartes' arguments involving clockwork and language:

If there were machines with the organs and appearance of a monkey, or some other irrational animal, we should have no means of telling that they were not altogether of the same nature as those animals; whereas if there were machines resembling our bodies, and imitating our actions as far as is morally possible, we should still have two means of telling that, all the same, they were not real men. First, they could never use words or other constructed signs as we do to declare our thoughts to others.[1]

When the giant king asks his learned men to decide what Gulliver is, they anticipate the Houyhnhnms' attack upon the normal human form as non-viable, and they also consider whether he may be an 'embrio or abortive birth' (chap. 3). This is perhaps an allusion to Locke's remark, 'It has more than once been debated, whether several human fœtus's should be preserved, or received to baptism, or no . . . The learned divine and lawyer, must, on such occasions, renounce his sacred definition of "animal rationale".' (III. vi. 26)

IV

Professor R. L. Colie has supplied the next link in my chain of data. In a brilliant note which appeared six years ago, Miss Colie pointed out what is probably the intellectual background of Swift's ape-man-horse seesaw (Yahoo-Gulliver-Houyhnhnm): this is a controversy between Edward Stillingfleet and John Locke over the nature of man.[2] In the *Essay* Locke had indeed defined reason as 'that faculty, whereby man is supposed to be distinguished from beasts, and wherein it is evident he much surpasses them'. (IV. xvii. 1) But Locke had also directly opposed himself to Descartes; for he argued that the signs of reason do appear in lower animals. When Stillingfleet, Bishop of Worcester,

[1] *Discourse on Method*, end of Pt. VI; trans. L. J. Lafleur (New York, 1950), p. 36. The argument is a recurrent one in Descartes' philosophical writings.

[2] See note 1, p. 18, above.

wrote a defence of the doctrine of the trinity, based upon traditional logic, he said that Locke's philosophy gave comfort to anti-trinitarians; and it was from this provocation that the quarrel arose.

Stillingfleet attacked Locke's explanation of the concept of man as a 'nominal essence'. He followed, instead, the traditional logical formula which had been rejected by the philosopher. According to this a creature is a man through enjoying a special 'subsistence' of the essence or nature peculiar to his species. Stillingfleet was blind to the problem which Locke dealt with: that since we do not directly know what the real essence of man or any other substance actually consists of, we cannot in practice use a 'subsistence' of it to identify examples of humanity; and so we must rely upon perceptible qualities. Benightedly, Stillingfleet wrote: 'The nature of a man is equally in Peter, James and John; and this is the common nature, with a particular subsistence, proper to each of them.' It is in virtue of this fact, according to Stillingfleet, that they are distinguished by separate, proper names: 'Peter, James and John are all true and real men.' [1]

Locke argued that if names not obviously human were employed, the bishop would be seen to be question-begging: e.g. if Locke should ask 'whether Weweena, Chuckery and Cousheda, were true and real men or no', Stillingfleet would not be able to tell. Then Locke continued:

Body, life, and the power of reasoning, being not the real essence of a man, as I believe your lordship will agree; will your lordship say, that they are not enough to make the thing, wherein they are found, of the kind called man, and not of the kind called baboon, because the difference of these kinds is real? If this be not real enough to make the thing of one kind and not of another, I do not see how *animal rationale* can be enough really to distinguish a man from an horse. [2]

Stillingfleet answered uncomprehendingly: 'Your Weweena, Cuchepy [sic] and Cousheda I have nothing to say to, they may be

[1] Quoted from Stillingfleet (*A Discourse in Vindication of the Doctrine of the Trinity*, 1697) by Locke, in his *A Letter to the . . . Bishop of Worcester* (1697), p. 195.

[2] *Works*, 5th ed. (1751), I, pp. 386–8 (reprinting Locke's *Letter to the . . . Bishop of Worcester*, 1697).

drills [i.e. baboons] for anything I know; but Peter, James and John are men of our own country.' [1]

In his reply, Locke discussed the names and natures of men and drills, and brought in the horse as well:

[Stillingfleet] says, that the nature of a man is equally in Peter, James and John. That's more than I know: Because I do not know what things Peter, James and John are. They may be drills, or horses, for ought I know . . . for I know a horse that was called Peter; and I do not know but the master of the same team might call other of his horses, James and John. Indeed, if Peter, James and John, are supposed to be the names only of men, it cannot be questioned but the nature of man is equally in them. . . . But then this to me, I confess, [seems] . . . to say no more but this, that a man is a man, and a drill is a drill, and a horse is a horse. [2]

The impenetrable Stillingfleet retorted that even the owner of the horse named Peter would disagree with Locke, would be able to tell the beast from a man, and would say, 'My man Peter and I can sit and chop logick together about our country affairs, and he can write and read, and he is a very sharp fellow at a bargain; but my horse Peter can do none of these things, and I never could find any thing like reason in him, and do you think I do not know the difference between a man and a beast?' [3] For fifteen (small octavo) pages Stillingfleet continued to show how one could tell a horse from a man and a man from a baboon (pp. 159–74).

To all this, Locke replied at greater length yet, demonstrating, for instance, that what seem to be necessary properties of the abstract concept of man may well be lacking in specific men:

Rationality as much a property as it is of a man, is no property of Peter; he was rational a good part of his life, could write and read, and was a sharp fellow at a bargain: But about thirty, a knock so altered him, that for these twenty years past, he has been able to do none of these things, there is to this day, not so much appearance of reason in him, as in his horse or monkey: and yet he is Peter still. [4]

---

[1] *The Bishop of Worcester's Answer to Mr. Locke's Letter* (1697), p. 120.

[2] *Works*, I, p. 425 (reprinting *Mr. Locke's Reply to the . . . Bishop of Worcester's Answer*, 1697, pp. 132–4).

[3] *The Bishop of Worcester's Answer to Mr. Locke's Second Letter* (1698), pp. 160–2.

[4] *Works*, I, p. 556 (reprinting *Mr. Locke's Reply to the . . . Bishop of Worcester's Answer to His Second Letter*, 1699, p. 358).

That Swift would have read Locke's polemical discourses appears probable. They were published while Swift, a studious young priest, was living at Moor Park with Sir William Temple, often visiting nearby London, and writing *A Tale of a Tub* and *The Battle of the Books*. Locke's and Stillingfleet's pamphlets belonged to the sensational trinitarian controversy which fulminated throughout the reign of William and Mary, shook Convocation, and provoked a royal edict. The Locke-Stillingfleet exchanges were among the most important and notorious contributions to this warfare. Locke's side of it was included, with the *Essay concerning Human Understanding*, in the first volume of his collected works (1714), so that whoever looked at this form of his masterpiece would find with it his three letters to Stillingfleet. There is little doubt that Swift would have followed the original trinitarian controversy, or that he read Locke's political and philosophical works. It seems likely, therefore, that he would have met these pamphlets. Even if he happened to miss them, however, their themes and terms were in the air for decades.[1]

V

How does this material—supposing it to be relevant—help us to understand Gulliver's last voyage? It does seem to imply that Swift's attack is made on the broadest possible front. The object ridiculed is not Europeans, Christians, Irish landlords, or the middle class; it is mankind. From the author's point of view, all the persons in the book, apart from the Yahoos and the Houyhnhnms, are examples of the general concept *human being*: the English seamen, the Lilliputians, the Blefescudians, the Brobdingnagians, the Dutch and Japanese pirates, the Laputans; the inhabitants of Balnibarbi, Luggnagg, Glubbdubdrib, and Japan;

---

[1] Swift once quoted from the book by Stillingfleet which started the controversy with Locke, the *Discourse in Vindication of the Doctrine of the Trinity*; see Swift's *Prose Works*, ed. H. Davis (Oxford, 1939–   ), II, p. 79. Swift once owned Stillingfleet's *A Rational Account of the Grounds of the Protestant Religion* (1681); see his *Correspondence*, I, p. 28. He also owned Stillingfleet's *Origines Sacrae*, 4th ed. (1675); see Sir Harold Williams, *Dean Swift's Library* (Cambridge, 1932), item no. 334 in the sale catalogue.

the Dutch seamen, the English mutineers, the savage islanders, the Portuguese seamen; Glumdalclitch, the King of Brobdingnag, Lord Munodi, and Captain Pedro de Mendez. Narrower classifications—religious, national, or social groups—would not seem to be the ultimate objects, therefore, of Swift's purely moral inquiry. The human characters have no common religion, nation, or class. The group of admirable characters—the King of Brobdingnag, Lord Munodi, Captain de Mendez—are not described as more or less religious than the others. The Houyhnhnms have no revealed faith at all. One cannot, apparently, regard the Houyhnhnms or Yahoos as opposed to men in religious terms. Rather the problem seems to be to induce from the assemblage of specimens of mankind a definition which will not only comprehend them but will distinguish them from Yahoos without granting them the properties of Houyhnhnms. At the same time the effect of the varied exhibit is to disprove the validity of current definitions.

Perhaps Swift is obliging his readers to acknowledge the paradox that most of them cling to a concept of their species which would exclude their respective selves. If he is following Locke, he may be further implying that 'man' as commonly used involves contradictory elements and could be split into a pair of 'nominal essences', excluding the irrational from the truly human; for Locke says, 'The idea of the shape, motion, and life of a man without reason, is as much a distinct idea, and makes as much a distinct sort of things from man and beast, as the idea of the shape of an ass with reason would be different from either that of man or beast, and be a species of an animal between, or distinct from both.' (IV. iv. 13) Against this background the Yahoos would embody an ironical reflection upon the fact that the bulk of unthinking men do in practice treat external shape as a sounder guide to humanity than reasonable conduct. Further yet, and as the bitterest irony of all, the Yahoos seem Swift's way of showing that for practical purposes one could more easily distinguish man by his vices than by his virtues; for it is certain vices, says Gulliver, that are 'rooted in the very souls of all my species' (letter to Sympson).

c

Contrariwise, by having the Houyhnhnms invariably act rationally, Swift defines reason so that men seem as irrational as possible. Professor Crane has shown that the common meaning of *animal rationale* was (implicitly) not an animal which in practice never diverged from reason, but one which had the power and tendency to behave rationally. By assuming that invariable rationality is the true significance of the word, Swift sharpens the satire: judged by that standard, we must all fail; and so the proper definition of man becomes limited to the class of beings like the King of Brobdingnag, who can act rationally and try to do so.

An apparent flaw in these hypotheses is that they make the Houyhnhnms out to be a positive ideal in spite of the passages where they appear absurd. To begin with, however, I do not suggest that the Houyhnhnms or any figures in the satire possess a consistent character. The voice throughout is that of Swift. He employs Gulliver and the other persons as either straightforward or ironical mouthpieces; and they have neither the independence, the consistency, nor the life of characters in a novel. Frequently, he gives them a coherent symbolic function; and he alludes to them of course as if they were people. But one cannot tell whether their actions and speeches are ironical or serious except by considering, not the relations of the characters within a narrative framework, but the implicit tone or attitudes of the author. The representation of the persons changes arbitrarily from ironical to serious as it happens to fit Swift's didactic aim.

There should be no doubt that Swift sometimes twists the Houyhnhnms' tails. One instance is the contempt thrown by Gulliver's master upon the human form divine: the flatness of our face, the prominence of our nose, etc. Not only is this attack comically hippocentric, but it recalls similar animadversions by Pliny, Plutarch, and a great train of followers.[1] Such attacks grew so frequent during the sixteenth century that Montaigne ridiculed 'ces plaintes vulgaires';[2] and Swift, if nothing else, knew Montaigne too well to be ignorant of his arguments. Behind the Houyhnhnms' fault-finding, we can see Swift wink at us.

[1] See Boas, *op. cit.*, passim.   [2] *Essais*, ed. Pierre Villey (Paris, 1930), II, p. 246.

If, then, the Houyhnhnms represent an ideal, why does the author joke at their expense? I suppose the comprehensive answer is that Swift was a joker. Like Shaw, he often could not resist a comic opening even when the indulgence would obscure a satirical design; and so he ridicules our own anthropocentricity in the Houyhnhnms. Some comedy is inevitable, moreover, when an author tries to produce beings which share the properties of a horse at the same time as they embody the highest natural virtues. The attempt is bound to collapse on one level or the other; and the collapse is bound to seem funny.[1] The more coherence we try to impose on the Houyhnhnms, the more awkward we make Swift's procedure. Yet I think one can accept them as ideal patterns where Swift is setting them off against man's irrationality, and as comic figures where he is smiling at the whole project of bestowing concrete life upon unattainable abstractions. Finally, the jokes may be Swift's method of ridiculing platitudinous moralists who, unlike himself, pose as Houyhnhnms. He is perhaps warning the sophisticated reader that this author, unlike Gulliver, appreciates the comical aspect of his own didacticism. It need not seem odd that a tough-minded evangelist should acknowledge the quixotry of his vocational ambition: to reform the human race.

Still, that the Houyhnhnms are not in themselves pleasing to the readers of our epoch, is hardly doubtful. Supposing there were no strength in any other criticism made of Swift by Huxley, Orwell, and their epigones, they would remain irrefutable witnesses of this failure. If, says Swift, we were more like the Houyhnhnms in character, we should be better off than we are now: that is his premise. And though his contemporaries, whether Protestant, Roman, or deist, spoke in unison with him, his readers today almost as single-mindedly shout *No*. Here flows, between them and us, the Styx to which I suspect Dr. Leavis was pointing when he said, 'We shall not find Swift remarkable for intelligence if we think of Blake'.[2] What indeed may mean everything to some of

[1] Sherburn, *op. cit.*, p. 93.
[2] 'The Irony of Swift', *Scrutiny*, II, 1934, p. 378.

us—'The road of excess leads to the palace of wisdom'—would have meant nothing to Swift.

Nevertheless, as an element in the satire, the work of the Houyhnhnms is to represent not Swift's ideals but the reader's. It is probable that Swift did mean to embody his own values in them; but that is a biographical fact. Their use in the satire is to be taken for granted, an obvious moral standard. As Professor Landa remarks, the principles embodied in the Houyhnhnms were normative for everyone, ideals beyond definition and beyond criticism, invoked universally to judge the faults of man.[1] But besides seeing that no moralist in Swift's own generation would have rejected his premise, we must also see that his own attitude toward it belongs outside *Gulliver's Travels*. In the design of the book, the Houyhnhnms stand for what we, rather than the middle-aged Dean, consider ideal. If we could re-cast them to shape the view of human possibility bequeathed to us by Blake, Kierkegaard, or Marx, Swift's final argument would still obtain. This is perhaps what T. S. Eliot meant when he called the conclusion of *Voyage to the Houyhnhnms* 'one of the greatest triumphs that the human soul has ever achieved'.[2]

If we proceed from Swift's line, we must still decide whether Gulliver's behaviour after conversion to the Houyhnhnms' rationality (as an ideal) is admirable or absurd. Surely, the author does not desire us to imitate him, to secede from our families, and to live in stables. Yet if the Houyhnhnms are admirable, one might assume that Gulliver was right to adopt what appears to be their view of humanity. To step out of this dilemma, we may admit that Gulliver's fate cannot be admirable in any simple sense, for it violates principles implied throughout the *Travels*— and taught by Swift in pamphlets, sermons, letters, and prayers. This step can be reconciled with the claim that the Houyhnhnms are wholly good if we decide they are not what we can directly copy, that our immediate examples live elsewhere. In judging this universal human inadequacy to be regrettable, one need not

[1] Landa, *op. cit.*, p. 352.
[2] 'Ulysses, Order, and Myth', *The Dial*, LXXV, November 1923, p. 481.

exempt Gulliver from it. He does not suppose he is free from it; for though he strives to imitate the Houyhnhnms, he never imagines he has become one. Neither does he make the opposite error of mistaking a horse's shape for the mark of a Houyhnhnm, since he laments the brutality of horses though honouring them for bearing the lineaments of his masters. It is the vision of the life of reason that nourishes his apparent misanthropy: unlike most men, Gulliver at least tries to be a 'true' man; and both this attempt and the humility which it implies endow him with the ground upon which he condemns the pride of those who have less insight.

At least some of the human characters in *Gulliver* are recommended as models for men to imitate: the King of Brobdingnag, Lord Munodi, and Pedro de Mendez. It may seem a crux in interpretation that when several good people come forth to be moral examples, another ideal, in the figure of the Houyhnhnms, should be presented as well. But there can hardly be a real conflict between human and non-human models. Unattainable ideals are regularly set before us by moral instructors, with intermediary examples to soften our despair. In England, during Swift's lifetime, the homiletic standard of Christian perfection was, for Anglicans, not more but less strenuous than the preachments of Gulliver. The Christian, unlike the natural man, could fulfil himself in another life, and could meanwhile look for God's improving grace to support his own will. Just as, on the theological level, spirit must always be at odds with flesh, so in the moral order, conscience can never stop battling with concupiscence; and no man dare hope for the natural serenity of a Houyhnhnm.[1] We may replace the equine symbol by what ideal we please: Swift's reproach is not alone that our conduct falls short of the mark within our reach, but as well that we regard the ultimate mark as attainable. We fail to approach the Brobdingnagians, and we suppose we can be Houyhnhnms.

Since Gulliver stands for any reader, his conduct after the final return to England means more than the story of an aberration.

[1] Norman Sykes, *From Sheldon to Secker* (Cambridge, 1959), pp. 176-8.

The ending of Molière's *Le Misanthrope* is another version of the same parable; for Swift may have been hinting that the influence upon Gulliver of the Houyhnhnms' ideal virtues is no more extravagant than the effects of a strict and perfect obedience to Christian ideals would be in an eighteenth-century society.[1] Swift is perhaps delivering a moral analogue of the religious paradox which opens *An Argument against Abolishing Christianity*—where he says that if men did in fact practise primitive Christianity, they would destroy what they suppose to be a precious civilisation. So at the close of *Gulliver's Travels*, we may suppose that he addresses himself to the latitudinarian, the sentimentalist, the Christian, the deist, and anybody else who might not only regard the character of a Houyhnhnm as admirable but also treat it as an easy ideal for humanity, and that to these he says, 'If you really lived by your avowed principles, you would uproot society as Gulliver wrecks his family'.

[1] Sherburn, *op. cit.*, p. 97.

INDEX

Swift's opinions or attitudes are indexed under separate headings, such as 'History', and not under his name; his connections with other people are indexed under their name, not his. Swift's works and anonymous works are listed by title; other works, by author or editor only; characters and places in Swift's works are listed generally under their own names and not under the work. Peers appear under their title or (if Norman) their Christian name.

169